NAPOLEON AND THE
RESTORATION OF THE BOURBONS

Thomas Babington Macaulay,
from an 1833 engraving by S. W. Reynolds, senior,
after the portrait by S. W. Reynolds, junior.

Thomas Babington Macaulay

NAPOLEON AND THE
RESTORATION OF THE BOURBONS

The completed portion of Macaulay's projected
*History of France, from the Restoration of the Bourbons
to the Accession of Louis Philippe*

Edited by Joseph Hamburger

LONGMAN

Longman Group Limited London

*Associated companies, branches and representatives
throughout the world*

This edition © Longman Group Limited 1977

First published 1977

ISBN 0 582 50827 4

Set in Monophoto Garamond
and printed in Great Britain by
William Clowes & Sons, Limited
London, Beccles and Colchester

CONTENTS

——————

v

ACKNOWLEDGEMENTS

We are grateful to the following for permission to reproduce copyright material:

Cambridge University Press for a number of small extracts from Vol. 1 and Vol. 2 of *The Letters of Thomas Babington Macaulay*, editor T. Pinney; Mr R. W. P. Cockerton and Mr W. M. Brooke-Taylor for permission to reproduce extracts from the letters of John Taylor; The National Trust and the Master and Fellows of Trinity College, Cambridge, for extracts from the 1852 shelflist of *Macaulay's Library*; Macmillan Administration (Basingstoke) Ltd., for a short extract from *Selection From The Correspondence of The Late Macvey Napier*, edited by his son Macvey Napier, by permission of Macmillan London and Basingstoke; the National Portrait Gallery (Archives), London for the frontispiece.

PREFACE

Macaulay's unfinished *History of France* is published here for the first time. The surviving pages of the work are probably all, or almost all, that Macaulay wrote of this history, which, had he completed it, would have been his first book. He planned it as a history of the Revolution of 1830, including its immediate background. The portion that he completed consists of an analysis of the Napoleonic regime and an account of the restored Bourbon regime from the collapse of the Empire to the Hundred Days. Thus the book has been given the title *Napoleon and the Restoration of the Bourbons*. It should be noted, however, that Macaulay's title, which does not accurately describe the portion he completed, was *The History of France, from the Restoration of the Bourbons to the Accession of Louis Philippe*.

Macaulay's narrative, here as in most of his historical writing, presents certain political themes, and these reveal something about his purposes as a politician. In addition, because of the presence of these themes Macaulay's writing may be considered a part of the literature of political theory. Thus there is evidence of his concern with the character of despotism, the causes and justification of revolution, the problem of legitimacy, and, above all, the problem of maintaining moderate regimes of the center which combine order and liberty and which avoid the extremes both of despotism, which seeks order but sacrifices liberty, and anarchy, which seeks liberty but sacrifices order. Discussion of such things was a reflection of his belief that the results of historical inquiry should be made available to politicians who faced problems for which there were historical parallels. Because these themes are interwoven with Macaulay's analysis of events in France, the unfinished history is more important for what it reveals about his manner of thinking about politics than for what it tells us about French history; therefore the introductory commentary emphasizes how his analysis of French politics reflects his political understanding as it was shaped by his observation of English developments.

Finding the unfinished *History* was the successful culmination of a search that took place intermittently during a period of about four years. As scrutiny of various collections of Macaulay papers led to negative results, a search was made for the papers of Dionysius Lardner, the editorial entrepreneur who invited Macaulay to write the history for the *Cabinet Cyclopaedia*. This led to the Longman archives, for Longmans, with John Taylor, had published the *Cabinet Cyclopaedia*. A visit was made to the archives at the University of Reading in the hope of finding in Longman's records of dealings with Lardner some clue to the next stage of inquiry. Examination of a list of books by Longman authors uncovered the entry, 'Macaulay, Thomas Babington. Elements of a History of France – unpublished. 1830.'

It is pleasing to record that my son Philip played an important part in finding the unfinished history. By asking probing questions and by prodding me to follow up improbable but conceivably fruitful clues after I had all but given up the search, he was instrumental in locating the document. Having played this role, it was especially appropriate that he was the one who found the reference to the unfinished history in the list of holdings. My sights were on a more modest target, and I was looking at business records for the *Cabinet Cyclopaedia* when Philip announced, with the voice of one who never doubted this result, 'Here it is.'

I am greatly indebted to Professors Robert Palmer and Stanley Mellon for their informative comments on Macaulay's text and my introduction. They have saved me from errors and have been most helpful in many ways. Without help from Dr Stephen Parks, Curator of the Osborn Collection at the Beinecke Library, Yale University, I would not have been able to draw the conclusions on the basis of bibliographical considerations which are discussed in the introduction. Indeed, he suggested the explanation of how the surviving printed pages originated.

Several others have been helpful. Eugenia and Robert Herbert offered many suggestions in aid of my search for the engraving that was planned as an illustration for Macaulay's book. Mr Neil Howe did most of the research and writing for the biographical glossary. Thomas Pinney was generous, as always, in responding to my inquiries. Miss J. Sinar, County Archivist at the Derbyshire Record Office, Mr J. A. Edwards, Archivist at Reading University Library, and Mr Trevor Kaye of Trinity College Library generously helped during my visits to their institutions.

Several persons and institutions have kindly allowed me to publish extracts of manuscripts in their possession, and I am glad to record my gratitude to them. Mr R. W. P. Cockerton, of Burre House, Bakewell and Mr W. M. Brooke-Taylor (papers of John Taylor); Derbyshire County Record Office at Matlock (papers of John Taylor); the National Trust for Places of Historic Interest and Natural

Beauty (the shelf list of Macaulay's library in 1852); the Master and Fellows of Trinity College, Cambridge (Macaulay's Journals); and Longman Group Ltd (miscellaneous ledgers and records, and the printed pages of Macaulay's *History of France*).

Some of the research required for the introduction was supported by grants from the Penrose Fund of the American Philosophical Society and the A. Whitney Griswold Faculty Research Fund at Yale University. I am glad to record my gratitude to both institutions for their generous help.

J.H.

INTRODUCTION

In 1876 Thomas Babington Macaulay's nephew and biographer, George Otto Trevelyan, reported the survival of the proofs of the first 88 pages of Macaulay's 'History of France, from the Restoration of the Bourbons to the Accession of Louis Philippe.' Trevelyan had seen the proofs at the Spottiswoode printing office.[1]* Even earlier, in 1862, one of Macaulay's earliest biographers, Frederick Arnold, having seen the work mentioned in the press of the early 1830s, suggested that 'the public would be pleased indeed by such a valuable and important fragment.'[2] But since the time of Trevelyan's report it has disappeared from general notice and has escaped scholars' searches, leading the late A. N. L. Munby to call it one of 'those *introuvables*' that brought despair to researchers and collectors.[3] The fragment published here is that described by Trevelyan in 1876.

Macaulay had planned the history as an analysis of the Revolution of 1830 and the events leading up to it, and he composed it during late 1830 and 1831. At age twenty-nine, Macaulay had just become a Member of Parliament. When he first formed his plan for a 'History of France' he had given his maiden speech on the civil disabilities of the Jews, but he had not yet given the speeches on reform that were to make him famous as a parliamentary orator. His reputation at this time mainly rested on his notable contributions to the *Edinburgh Review*. His articles on Milton, Canning's coalition, Hallam, and James Mill displayed verve and erudition, and they presented a political outlook that was thoughtful, even speculative, and yet which also had a bearing on the politics of the day. It was said that the articles on James Mill and the Benthamites led Lord Lansdowne to offer Macaulay his pocket borough of Calne. To some, of course, he was also known as the son of Zachary

Macaulay, the spokesman for the Evangelicals, especially on the anti-slavery question. And to some he was also known for his achievements at Trinity College, Cambridge, and as a speaker at the Union Society. But above all, it was through his important articles in the *Edinburgh Review* that Macaulay had achieved prominence in 1830, identifying him as a man of letters and a political writer of note. Of course, this was a far cry from the fame that came later from his service in India, his achievement of a leading position in the Whig party, and his *History of England*, but in 1830, although not yet at this pinnacle of fame, the signs of future eminence were discernible.

Had it not been for Henry Brougham, Macaulay's writing on France would have been somewhat different, and it would not have disappeared from view. Soon after the July Revolution, like many others in England, Macaulay was eager to go to France to observe events at first hand. He also planned to write an article about French politics for the *Edinburgh Review*. The article, as he described it to Macvey Napier, the editor, would have been 'on the politics of France since the Restoration, with characters of the principal public men, and a parallel between the present state of France and that of England.' He warned that it would be quite long, and although he made no immodest claims for it, he was confident that it would be 'an article of extraordinary interest.'[4] On 1 September he sailed for Dieppe on his first continental journey, carrying with him Napier's approval of his proposal for the article.

Napier and Macaulay had not counted on Brougham, who also planned an article on French politics. Brougham's claims on the *Review* were considerable. He had been present at its founding in 1802 and had been the most prolific contributor, being responsible for as many as four articles in some of its quarterly numbers. In addition, as one of the leading spokesmen for the Whigs in Parliament, he often wrote articles to shape opinion and to muster support for the Whig cause – or for his own view of that cause. The article on France was to be no exception. When he told Napier that he intended to 'make a point of giving . . . my thoughts on the Revolution,' he explained that 'all our movements next session turn on that pivot, and I can trust no one but myself with it, either in or out of Parliament.' Indeed, he insisted that his should be the lead article, and he imperiously told Napier to 'send off your countermand to Macaulay,' which the editor promptly did.[5]

Macaulay was furious. He had turned down another offer to write on French affairs, and he had thrown away the labor of a month. Writing, as he later admitted, 'in haste and warmth,' he severed his connection with the *Edinburgh Review*. He did not blame Napier; on the contrary, he acknowledged that any editor of the *Review* would be obliged to yield to Brougham's demands, for to refuse them would risk ruining the publication. This was hard on Macaulay's pride and the chief cause of his anger. He and Brougham were not on easy terms. Brougham had long enjoyed success and prominence: eminently successful at the bar, to which Macaulay could bear witness, as they both travelled on the Northern Circuit; a leader of his party in the House of Commons, where he had served since 1810; a prolific pamphleteer and publicist since 1802; and an active supporter, indeed often leader, in public causes, including the anti-slavery movement, in which he cooperated with Macaulay's father, who appreciated and even venerated Brougham.

Macaulay, on the other hand, was at the beginning of a career in which he could hope for eminence in both literature and politics at least as great as that enjoyed by Brougham and perhaps more deserved. Confident about his own talent, and resentful of Brougham's slights and condescension, he was hypercritical of what he regarded as Brougham's undeserved reputation. Brougham, he said, '*half knows* every thing from the cedar to the hyssop.'[6] Their mutual suspicions became most evident in connection with the *Edinburgh Review*. They were often in competition for favored subjects and for public favor. Brougham complained about the length of Macaulay's review of Hallam and about the substance of his articles on the Canning coalition and on James Mill and the Benthamites. He also opposed the proposal made by Francis Jeffrey, as retiring editor of the *Edinburgh Review*, that Macaulay be his successor. Macaulay, on his side, noting that Brougham 'became extremely cold to me,' explained that Brougham 'felt that his power over the Review diminished as mine increased.' Macaulay suggested that it was jealousy which Brougham regularly felt for those who were political allies and even friends but who demonstrated promise of achieving eminence, thereby threatening to eclipse Brougham himself.[7] Furthermore, Macaulay's resentment was accentuated by obligations to Brougham, who had shown interest in Macaulay's career and who, as recently as 1828, had recommended to the Lord Chancellor Macaulay's appointment as a Commissioner of Bankrupts, a post that was welcomed as it brought in almost £300 annually.

Against this immediate background of rivalry and resentment it is not surprising to find Macaulay reacting with 'haste and warmth' when he learned that Napier had yielded to Brougham's demand. Brougham, he said, was 'the person of all persons on earth to whose dictation I feel least inclined to stoop. Your intentions towards me,' he told Napier, 'I know, are perfectly kind and fair. I have no such confidence with respect to his. I would sacrifice much to your convenience. But I cannot tell you how my whole heart and soul rise up against the thought of sacrificing any thing to his love of domination.' Brougham was pictured as thinking of himself as 'a man who act[s] a prominent part in the world: he [Macaulay] is nobody.' And Napier was told that

> no man likes to be reminded of his inferiority in such a way: and there are some particular circumstances in this case which render the admonition more unpleasant than it would otherwise be. I know that Brougham dislikes me; and

I have not the slightest doubt that he feels great pleasure at having taken this subject out of my hands, and at having made me understand, – as I do most clearly understand, – how far my services are rated below his.

The incident made the connection with the *Edinburgh Review* 'a source of humiliation and mortification.'[8]

In the end Macaulay stayed within the fold and became the most admired and the most highly valued of contributors to the *Review*. Meanwhile he had already made alternative arrangements for the publication of his writing on France. The offer he had turned down was from Dionysius Lardner, editor and one of the proprietors of the *Cabinet Cyclopaedia*.[9] (The other proprietors were Longmans and John Taylor,[10] best known as publisher and friend of Keats and John Clare.) Lardner's offer was repeated in October 1830, and Macaulay agreed to write 'an account of the political changes of France since the Restoration and of this late revolution.'[11] Macaulay's contract has not survived, but judging by payments made by the *Cabinet Cyclopaedia* to comparable authors, Macaulay probably would have received no more than £200.[12] Had it been published, the French history would have been his first book.

In the fragment that is here published for the first time Macaulay dealt with two historical episodes – the Napoleonic regime as the immediate background to the restoration, and the restoration of Louis XVIII in 1814, including an analysis of the difficulties Louis faced as he tried to gain support for his regime. This is considerably less than Macaulay had planned for his book, for his intention was to focus on the events of 1830 and to include as background an account of the fifteen years preceding the revolution. Evidently Lardner thought of it as a supplement to Eyre Evans Crowe's *History of France*, also published in the *Cabinet Cyclopaedia*, which ended with the fall of Napoleon's empire in 1814.[13] Thus Macaulay did not provide accounts of Louis's reign after Waterloo, the reign of Charles X, or of the July revolution. Most of this probably was never written, although Macaulay, while still believing that his work would appear in the *Edinburgh Review*, and acting on Napier's suggestion, had begun work on the events of 1830.[14] Whatever he wrote on this has not yet been found.

What survives of Macaulay's *History* was written between August 1830 and November 1831, and almost all of it was written by June 1831.[15] After it became clear that he could not publish in the *Edinburgh Review*, he turned to the historical background to the Revolution. Already in October 1830 he hoped to finish by Christmas, and he appears to have been working intensively on it in January 1831, judging by Francis Jeffrey's hope that he finish so 'that he will soon be restored to his disconsolate friends.' He seems to have been under pressure of a deadline in March, for he apologized to Napier for not having an article for the next number of the *Review*, explaining that he had 'put off the History of [Fr]ance to the last moment,' and that whatever time he could spare from the House of Commons would be devoted to the volume for Lardner.[16]

Anticipating early completion of the work, Longmans, as publisher (in addition to being co-proprietor with Taylor and Lardner), commissioned the making of an engraving for the illustration that was to appear on the title-page. It was to be a vignette of Arcole, the name adopted by a hero in the street fighting that took place in Paris in July 1830.[17] The engraver, Edward Finden, was paid £27–6–0 as early as 2 February 1831; the engraving was based on a drawing by Henry Corbould.[18] By October 6,000 title-pages were produced.[19] Meanwhile, Macaulay had submitted the first installment; this was probably in May, for on 1 June a copyist had been paid to produce a legible copy for the printer, and later in June the author was receiving proofs.[20] Throughout this period and for about two years or so beyond the work was being advertised.[21]

Although most and perhaps all of the fragment published here was in proof in June 1831, Macaulay worked on the history during the next few months. In October he told Napier that Lardner 'is very desirous to bring out my book about France – and I wish to finish at least the first part of it for him, before I do any thing else.' Soon after this all mention of it disappears from surviving correspondence, although advertisements of the work continued to appear. It will be noted that Macaulay referred to the 'first part' of the work, indicating that it was to appear in two volumes.[22] This suggests that he was finding it difficult to confine his treatment of the subject to the size of book originally planned. This is also evident in the fragment that survives, for it ends on proof page 89,[23] yet its narrative terminates with the allies' entry into Paris after the battle of Waterloo.

It seems unlikely that Macaulay wrote more on the historical background to the Revolution of 1830 than has survived (except, of course, for the small number of missing pages). Therefore it is necessary to dispute G. O. Trevelyan's inference from a marginal note in the fragment 'to the effect that most of the type was broken up before the sheets had been pulled.'[24] The words that Trevelyan evidently saw were, 'Distributed. (greater part before it was pulled.).' This notation appears in the head margin of the first page. Trevelyan, apparently assuming that this statement referred to the entire fragment, inferred that most of what Macaulay had written had been lost. However, he could not have made this inference if he had examined the analogous notations on the first pages of each of the gatherings that followed, for the fact that such notations were made for each of those gatherings indicates that the marginal notation that appeared to support Trevelyan's inference applied only to the first sixteen pages. And indeed, it is true that the "greater part' of the type used for the first sheet was distributed before it was pulled, for it is only pages 1, 8, 9, and 16 that have survived. Although some type was distributed from the pages that made up the surviving sheets, distribution had not proceeded so far that it was necessary to make similar notations with regard to the other gatherings. Thus on the first pages of each of the other gatherings there is only a notation indicating that the type had been distributed, but there is no indication that distribution had occurred before sheets had been pulled (except the second gathering where the notation states that '19 & 20 in part [distributed] before being pulled').

These considerations cast doubt on Trevelyan's suggestion that most of what Macaulay had written had been destroyed. There is yet other evidence, however, that the surviving printed pages are all or almost all that Macaulay wrote. For one thing, what follows page 80 appears to be proof copy made for the purpose of identifying and correcting errors in composition, and we may assume that the part in this stage of proof was what had been most recently written.[25] (The first eighty pages were printed for a different purpose, which will be discussed presently.) In addition, the note in the tail margin of page 80 stating that the '8 pages beyond this not imposed' strongly suggests that the pages of proof following page 80 were all the printer possessed, for had there been more, this marginal note would have specified a different number. Also, it should be noted that the type for the last line of the fragment is set in a way that suggests that the compositor had run out of manuscript. The page is incomplete, consisting of twenty-four lines, and the last of these, since there were insufficient words to occupy the entire line, is completed with an elongated ellipsis. Furthermore, it is arguable that the last paragraph has a summary character and shows signs of having been written hurriedly. Finally, Macaulay in his correspondence did not reveal a continuing concern with his French History, although observations about his writing often found their way into his letters. We know that he was correcting proof for gathering E (specifically page 63 in the fragment) in June 1831 and that in October he was too busy with the history to promise more than a short article on Bunyan for the *Edinburgh Review*. Possibly at this later time he was writing the part that survived as proof (the pages following page 80) and conceivably also the part that became gathering F (pages 65–80). However, by December, with the House of Commons recessed, he had 'leisure to think about the Edinburgh Review.' But the history was not mentioned. And in June 1832 he boasted of being 'a gentleman at large; and my employments are, reading Indian history and politics and writing for the Edinburgh Review.'[26] Trevelyan's suggestion that what survives is only a fragment of what Macaulay had written is probably incorrect. It is only a fragment of what had been planned, but (apart from what he wrote about the events of 1830 while still in Paris) probably it is the entirety of what he had written.

6

In considering why the book was not finished, in addition to the magnitude of the task, the demands made on Macaulay as a politician appear to have been mainly responsible. Initially he seemed able to combine his varied activities as prolific writer for the *Edinburgh Review*, as Commissioner of Bankrupts, as member of Parliament who suffered late sittings of the House, and as dutiful son and brother, though he did complain in December 1830 that 'my French History, the House of Commons, and the Bankrupts, have almost killed me between them.'[27] The pace of political life intensified in 1831, as the Reform Bill was introduced and popular agitation increased. Macaulay was deeply involved in these developments. He made important speeches on 2 March, 5 July, 20 September, 10 October, and 16 December. He took part in attempts to organize backbench pressure on the Ministry. He also wrote five articles for the *Edinburgh Review* during the approximately fourteen months while he was working on the book for Lardner.[28] In addition, during this period he mourned the deaths of his sister Jane and his mother. Yet all this did not prevent his working on the *History*. However, thanks to his splendid speeches on reform, Macaulay was becoming a leading spokesman for his party. The distractions and the demands grew, and soon the French history was to be put aside. Even though his office as one of the Commissioners of Bankrupts was abolished in January 1832, Macaulay, still engrossed in parliamentary politics and facing the prospect of an election contest at Leeds, was given a minor but demanding appointment in the government. In June 1832 he was made a member of the Board of Control for India and he was also appointed to a committee of inquiry into the East India Company charter, which was to expire the following year. Macaulay became actively involved in the work that led to the government's recommendations for the revision of the charter, and at this time he also won his seat at Leeds. So fully engaged in parliamentary, electoral and Indian affairs, and soon to go to India as Law Member of the Governor General's Council, he seems to have neglected the French *History*.

It remains to speculate how the surviving printed pages were made and to describe how these pages reached the archives of Longman Group Ltd, where they are now preserved. Of the 89 octavo pages on which the fragment was printed, pages 1–80, unlike the pages following, were not proofs made for corrections, for we know that in June 1831 when he was correcting proofs Macaulay was defending the formulation of a sentence which was altered before the surviving copy was printed.[29] Although not proofs, pages 1–80 could not have been made in the course of normal commercial production, for, as we know from marginal notes in the fragment, the pages were pulled despite there being missing parts (pages 2–7, 10–15, 35, and parts of 19 and 20).[30] It is the missing parts, which are explained by the marginal notes indicating that type for some pages had been distributed before the pages were pulled, that suggest the circumstances in which the fragment was saved from complete obliteration. It is clear that the surviving pages were pulled by someone who wished to save this fragment of Macaulay's writing from destruction despite the missing pages caused by distribution of type. One can visualize someone at the Spottiswoode printing office who knew of Macaulay as an essayist and parliamentary orator. Having seen the order to distribute the type, presumably because it became evident that the author would not complete the book, this hypothetical person tried to rescue a portion of the unfinished history. Since Macaulay's book was still being advertised in 1834, it may have been soon after this date that the standing type was broken-up. In entering the workroom where the distribution of type had already begun, our hypothetical rescuer pulled sheets from the imposed pages and folded them, thus putting together pages 1–80 of the fragment we now have.[31] This fragment was combined with the surviving pages of the separately preserved portion of page proof (pages 81–89), and at a later date they were bound together to form the volume which survives in the Longman archives.

Incomplete and only partially corrected, these surviving fragments were for many years kept at the offices of the printing firm of A. and R. Spottiswoode, which did much but not all of the printing for the *Cabinet Cyclopaedia*. There they remained unnoticed until 1860 when George Andrew Spottiswoode, perhaps reminded of their presence by Macaulay's recent death and his burial in Westminster Abbey, attached a note to them identifying the proofs as 'the fragment of Macaulay's France,' adding that 'no one but myself, I believe, now knows anything about it.' The next indication that anyone was aware of the existence of the proofs came from G. O. Trevelyan in his biography of Macaulay, published in 1876. There he noted that 'ten years ago proofs of the first eighty-eight pages were found in Messrs. Spottiswoode's printing office.'[32]. He did not make clear when he saw the proofs.

From Spottiswoode's the unfinished history was sent to Longmans. This was not inappropriate, for Longmans, as one of Lardner's co-proprietors and as publisher of the *Cabinet Cyclopaedia*, had ordered the printing from Spottiswoode, and after 1851 Longmans was the sole proprietor of the series.[33] Furthermore, as publisher of Macaulay's famous *History of England* and other works, it was fitting that George Andrew Spottiswoode, who was Thomas Longman's cousin, should send the printed but unpublished pages. The date of the transfer is unknown, but it was probably accomplished by 1879, for the first of the binder's leaves, which served as the flyleaf, bears the signature of Thomas Longman IV (1804–79), who died during that year. Indeed, one may speculate that the transfer was made after the appearance of Trevelyan's biography in 1876, which brought renewed prominence to Macaulay and his connection with Longmans. Since Longmans' premises in Paternoster Row were destroyed by fire in 1863, had the transfer been made much earlier, the fragment might not have survived. Longmans made a slim volume of it, and judging by the binding and by the presence of the signature of Thomas Longman IV, it would seem that it was bound at about this time (1876–79). And it has been in the Longman archives that the unfinished history has remained to this day.

For some years before he began writing about France, Macaulay was interested in the character of historical inquiry and had some clearly defined ideas about it, at least some of which we should expect to find reflected in his unfinished *History of France*. History, Macaulay believed, should serve politics by teaching politicians and citizens how to maintain a moderate, constitutional regime in which both liberty and order are preserved, each balanced against the other, and neither promoted to the neglect of the other. This meant that the political center had to be protected by politicians who opposed extremist parties on both sides of the political spectrum, for at the extremes one found doctrinairism, zeal, and fanaticism on behalf of policies that would lead, in one direction, to anarchy, or, in the other, to despotism. The extremes could be diminished and the center defended, Macaulay held, by making adjustments in institutions in response to demands for change, and by making concessions to those who had grievances.

History could help in the defense of the political center by pointing to the way that policies had worked out in the past, so that politicians might endorse or avoid comparable policies in their own time. Charles I, for example, did not alter his conception of the monarchy to take account of intellectual and social changes that had occurred: 'he would govern the men of the seventeenth century as if they had been the men of the sixteenth century; and therefore it was, that all his talents and all his virtues did not save him from . . . civil war, . . . from a scaffold. These things,' Macaulay added, 'are written for our instruction.' Pointing to Ireland, he said, 'Remember how, in that country, concessions too long delayed were at last received. That great boon [Catholic emancipation] which in 1801, in 1813, in 1825, would have won the hearts of millions, given too late, and given from fear, only produced new clamours and new dangers.' And he asked, 'Is not one such lesson enough for one generation?' Or, to take one of his French examples, and still urging timely concession with regard to parliamentary reform, Macaulay observed that 'It was because the French aristocracy resisted reform in 1783, that they were unable to resist revolution in 1789 . . . They would not endure Turgot: and they had to endure Robespierre.'[34] Thus Macaulay held that history 'is full of useful and precious instruction when we contemplate it in large portions,' and he insisted that it was the historian's 'office . . . to supply statesmen with examples and warnings.'[35]

When Macaulay turned to French history he looked for illustrations of themes that were at the heart of his own historical and political thinking. As in his view of seventeenth-century England, France exemplified the problems created by civil conflict and by a succession of regimes that were either despotic or anarchic, each, respectively, promoting order by sacrificing liberty, or promoting liberty by sacrificing order. Even the government set up by Louis XVIII in 1814 was analyzed from Macaulay's point of view, for he portrayed it as a regime that attempted to overcome the legacies of Bourbon absolutism, revolutionary anarchy, and Napoleonic despotism by establishing a constitution under which diverse groups might coexist. Although its failure disappointed Macaulay, he was able to analyze it with principles that he habitually used when interpreting English politics, whether as historian or as politician, for he regarded France under the Restoration, like nineteenth-century England, as having a moderate, centrist regime that was struggling against extreme factions on both sides of the political spectrum that were seeking to undermine it. Of course, Macaulay's tendency to interpret developments in France in terms of English experience – which was not uncommon amongst the French themselves – had its dangers. Fortunately for Macaulay, his most important interpretive themes were not irrelevant to French politics in 1814.

In the first part of the unfinished *History*, Macaulay analyzed Napoleon's regime, and this gave him an opportunity to discuss despotism. This part was supposed to have been prefatory to an account of the period beginning with the Restoration in 1814, but it contributes about half of the surviving portion of the *History*. He had also written about other oppressive regimes, especially in several accounts of the Stuarts, and was to do so again, most notably in his *History of England*. But compared with Napoleon, the Stuarts, although somewhat despotic, were only intermittently and less severely oppressive. The English nation, Macaulay explained, was at heart friendly to royalty; it acted as a friend does during a quarrel; although loving liberty, it had not forgotten its loyalty (67)*. Indeed, the government of Charles I, 'though in many things unconstitutional, had in one point only been cruelly oppressive...[that is, with regard to] religious opinions.... In spite of the illegal proceedings of the Stuarts, the civil government had been in the main good. The ecclesiastical government had been intolerable' (45).[36] In contrast to Stuart oppression, Napoleon, 'an artful tyrant,' designed 'to make up a despotism of the purest and most unmingled kind' (50).

Macaulay's account of Napoleonic France reflects his thinking about despotism, which was one of the most important categories in his thinking about history and politics. As early as 1822, in his 'Essay on the Life and Character of William III', with which he won the Greaves Prize at Trinity College, Cambridge, Macaulay briefly outlined a theory of history and politics that continued to shape his thinking throughout his life. Assuming that social and political conflict would normally take

---

References relate to pages in this book.

place, Macaulay held that the antagonists tended to become increasingly extreme, doctrinaire, zealous, even fanatical. At one extreme were the discontented who were angry and opposed to the established order. Their opposition, undertaken in the name of liberty, when pushed to the extreme would lead to anarchy. On the other side of the spectrum were the established classes who were mainly moved by fear. They acted in the name of order, but when pushed to the extreme, they became oppressive and established despotism.

Neither condition could be permanent, Macaulay argued, for each provoked its opposite. 'Each is the cause and the effect of its antagonist. Since the first recorded origin of government they have followed each other in perpetual succession.' On the one side, those too zealous to secure social order destroy liberty and provoke the use of 'the arts of vengeance' and 'the enthusiasm of despair,' leading to 'the fury of a multitude – the swords of Janissaries, – the daggers of assassins, – such are the instruments to which despotism drives its victims, and exposes its possessors.' However, once dominant, the opponents of despotism create anarchy, and this reverses the swing of the pendulum. The 'misguided friends' of liberty institute too much change, and this 'leads them to outrage the moral sense of mankind.' Thus 'it is by changes too violent for the temper of a people, by excessive vengeance for past abuses,' that liberty is endangered. Such things 'alarm the timid, disgust the good, and drive a nation to seek in slavery a refuge from commotion,'[37] Consequently, there is oscillation between anarchy and despotism, and 'states move on in the same eternal cycle, which, from the remotest point, brings them back again to the same sad starting-post.'[38]

There was an alternative to the cycle in which anarchy and despotism alternated, and this was a regime in which the extremes were minimized and the center preserved. In it there would be harmony and equilibrium, and society would be in that 'happy central point in which alone it can repose.' There would be an optimum combination of order and liberty, as each coexisted with the other, neither immoderately pursued to the exclusion of its opposite. England since 1688 enjoyed this fortunate situation, and Macaulay also regarded France at the time of the Restoration of the Bourbons in 1814 as attempting to establish such a regime.

Much more typical, however, was the situation before 1688 when the various parts of government were in a state, 'not of equilibrium but of alternate elevation and depression.'

> The tyranny of Charles the first produced civil war and anarchy. Anarchy in turn generated tyranny. Tyranny had now again produced resistance and revolution. And, but for the wisdom of the new King [William III], it seems probable that the same cycle of misery would have been again described.[39]

This interpretation was retained three decades later when the *History of England* appeared.[40] And Macaulay discerned the same swing of the pendulum in French history where the oppressive Bourbon regime was replaced by the anarchy of revolution, only to be followed by Napoleonic despotism.

When briefly describing the revolutionary period in the unfinished *History* Macaulay portrayed it as a period of increasing anarchy which culminated in Jacobin rule (48). The violence of revolution was a reaction that was proportional to the amount of oppression that had preceded. Thus the Revolution was described as having been extremely violent and anarchic: there were 'a succession of insurrections' (46); the public mind was in 'that fluctuating and agitated state in which a deep and searching revolution leaves it'; 'fundamental laws [were] as transitory as the fashions of apparel'; indeed, 'there was nothing certain in the state' (48). There was a limit, however, to the duration of revolution. The people were 'sick of incessant change' (48). Finally came the 9th of Thermidor, the fall of Robespierre, which was a turning point, for it was the first day since 1789 on which those who wished to stop the Revolution gained a decisive advantage over those who wished to propel it (46). 'The fury of the revolution had spent itself. The work of destruction was done. The old society had passed away, and the new creation commenced' (46).

The character and the severity of Napoleon's regime arose from its being a 'despotism sprung from a revolution' (58). Napoleon having 'announced himself as the champion at once of the revolution and of social order' (48), his regime, however authoritarian, had something of a liberal aspect. But despite Napoleon's support for religious toleration, a uniform administration, and the code (58), Macaulay regarded him as a despot who used a liberal façade to disguise his despotic intentions. Sieyès's plan for a constitution, for example, was used to appease suspicions nourished by what remained of the republican spirit which made it 'necessary that, for a time at least, the rising despotism should be veiled by the semblance of a constitution' (50). Indeed, far from allowing the liberal aspects of the regime to qualify his judgment, Macaulay recognized that they made the despotism more extreme. Thus he observed that by the abolition of the old system of administration Napoleon's power was enhanced:

> the executive power, instead of being checked – as it is checked in many of those monarchies which we call absolute, – by bodies strong in ancient prescription and in the habitual veneration of the people, had at its command a vast army of public functionaries selected by itself, paid by itself, removable at its pleasure, and expecting promotion only from its favour (53).

It was the same with his replacements for the old ecclesiastical establishment and the old aristocracy; by establishing new institutions dependent on himself, Napoleon not only gained new sources of support, but he also avoided dependence on bodies that had different loyalties and a measure of independence. Macaulay recognized that the continuation of some revolutionary measures, like the Revolution itself, left, so to speak, a clean slate on which Napoleon could design institutions that would be agreeable to his purposes. The result, had Napoleon's plans succeeded, 'would have renewed, perhaps for centuries, the expiring lease of tyranny.' For the feudal monarchy of the Bourbons he would have substituted 'a monarchy on the more simple pattern of the east.' Indeed, 'it is scarcely possible to estimate the amount of evil which he would have produced' (60).[41]

Napoleon went far towards his goal. With extraordinary talents and a despotic temperament, he approached his task systematically. A legislature was established that was 'the ready tool of arbitrary power'; a bureaucracy was created that was his instrument; all clergymen were his stipendiaries; a new aristocracy was created that derived its dignity and its very existence 'from the preference of the sovereign'; and the immense and magnificent army was a formidable instrument at Napoleon's command; and finally education was controlled and censorship provided because 'in an age in which opinion is all-powerful, despotism must have its foundation in falsehood' (53–57). The result was that all power and all institutions were 'virtually united in a single hand' (55). Furthermore, because of the revolution, 'young as his power was, it was more ancient than any of the other institutions of the state, and was the source, and the only source, of them all' (55). Macaulay noticed the contrast between England, where even amidst change many old practices and traditions survived, and France, where the pre-revolutionary society seemed to have been destroyed and replaced by institutions designed by Napoleon. This contrast allowed Macaulay to say that, 'In England the nation was something: in France, the government was every thing' (58).

Systematic though Napoleon's despotism was, in the end, his plans 'could not succeed'. Just as anarchy, when carried too far, would provoke a swing of the pendulum towards despotism, the same swing, but in the opposite direction, was brought on by the extreme of despotism. Of course military collapse had much to do with Napoleon's fall, but Macaulay also pointed to internal weakness. The extent of despotism stimulated 'a spirit of opposition' (61). And after the invasion, there was a failure of will. 'The emperor appealed in vain to that national spirit which he had broken, and was astonished not to find the self-devotion of freemen in those whom it had been the aim of his whole policy to tame down into slaves' (63). Even with the government threatened with destruction there might have been loyalty to the nation which transcended the particular government of the day. But under Napoleon, as Macaulay explained, the government was everything and the nation was nothing. Thus Napoleon found that 'the nation, that impetuous and warlike nation, which, twenty years before, had triumphed over Europe, amidst misrule, bankruptcy, and famine, seemed to have disappeared from the face of the earth' (63).

With the fall of Napoleon the pendulum swung away from despotism. However, it did not swing fully to the other extreme, for the regime established in 1814 with the return of Louis XVIII was portrayed by Macaulay as neither despotic nor anarchic. This did not mean that it was from Macaulay's point of view an ideal regime, for it had great difficulty in maintaining itself as a regime of the center, and in the end it failed. However, although unstable, it struggled against those who tried to subvert it, against those who wanted Napoleon's return, and those who longed for a complete restoration of the pre-1789 regime, and those that looked for a republican regime such as prevailed under the banners of the Revolution. This struggle occupied the second half of Macaulay's unfinished *History*.

Macaulay makes it clear that although a Bourbon was restored in 1814, the regime that was established was not a restoration of the old Bourbon monarchy. That would have been impossible, for too much had been altered.

> Louis returned to a people who knew not him nor his house. The France in which he had again set his foot was not that France which he had formerly known. The violent and searching revolution, which had driven him into exile, had, during his absence, done the work of ages.... A new people – new in their opinions, their prejudices, and their social relations, – had sprung into existence (68).

These circumstances were recognized by Louis, for in his Charter, although he defended his royal prerogative, in practice he provided guarantees of the liberties that were expected by those who had been shaped by the republican ideals of the revolutionary period (78–81).

As a regime of the center, Restoration France, like England with its constitution, was subjected to centrifugal forces that pulled it towards both anarchy and despotism. Therefore, as in England, its politics could be analyzed with concepts that were derived from the historical and political theory that Macaulay had made the main theme of his early essay on William III. According to this theory, the distinguishing characteristic of a center regime was its continuing struggle to restrain and undermine the extremist tendencies in order to bring itself to 'that happy central point in which alone it can repose.' Yet the push to the extremes was always present, even under stable governments. Social, economic, religious, intellectual change – what Macaulay called noiseless revolutions – made it inevitable. Such changes created discontents which stimulated the growth of radicalism and perhaps rebellion, and those who were not dissatisfied experienced fear as they discerned a threat of anarchy. Unwilling to be conciliatory, their response was to repress, which, on the opposite side, created anger among the radicals who then discerned a threat of despotism.

It was the task of the politician to arrest these tendencies in order to preserve the center. From this point of view the extremist was the enemy, and Macaulay consistently expressed his loathing for the sectarian, the zealot, the fanatic. Furthermore, the extremist was objectionable on whichever side of the political spectrum he resided. 'There are those who will be contented with nothing but demolition; and there are those who shrink from all repair. There are innovators . . . and there are bigots.' Or, in another formulation, he said,

> Fanatics of one kind might anticipate a golden age, in which men should live under the simple dominion of reason, in perfect equality and perfect amity, without property, or marriage, or king, or God. A fanatic of another kind might see nothing in the doctrines of the philosophers but anarchy and atheism, might cling more closely to every old abuse, and might regret the good of old days . . .[42]

Since each extreme provoked the growth of its opposite, both had to be opposed.

The politician was to defend the center by being a mediator between the aggrieved who demanded change and the complacent who resisted it. The emphasis was on finding remedies for reasonable grievances, on soothing the public mind, on reconciliation of differences, and on averting civil discord. The politician was to exercise his art by offering timely concessions – the timeliness serving to appease the aggrieved before radical leaders gained their support. 'The true source of the power of demagogues,' Macaulay noted, 'is the obstinacy of rulers,' and he added, 'a liberal Government makes a conservative people.' This was 'true statesmanship' – guiding public opinion to the support of those modest changes that extended and made firmer the consent for the existing constitutional order. It may be noted that Macaulay was recommending that the politician draw something from both extremes: in response to those demanding change he acknowledged that some reform was necessary, and in response to those resisting change he acknowledged that the existing order ought to be defended. Thus he could say, 'Reform that you may preserve.'[43]

The justification for this policy of preserving the center was that it would reduce the threat of despotism that came from those who would bring 'exclusion, persecution, severe punishment for libellers and demagogues, proscriptions, massacres, civil war, if necessary, rather than any concessions to a discontented people.'[44] His policy would reduce the threat of anarchy from the opposite side, from which 'would come agitation, tumult, political associations, libels, inflammatory harangues.'[45] Although each of these alternatives were in themselves evil, by steering a course between them the politician also was reducing the possibility of civil war. Alternatively by defending the center against one side consisting of 'the enemies of all order' and, on the other, of 'the enemies of all liberty,' it became possible to have a constitutional order in which liberty and order were combined.[46]

This conception of the purpose of politics informed Macaulay's political judgments during the decade that preceded his writing on France – and, for that matter, throughout his life. He tried to find middle ground between Mitford's extreme opposition to democracy and James Mill's dogmatic defense of it. During the period of the Canning ministry he searched for a middle position between the policy of the ultra-Tories and radicalism. He continued to do this during the Reform Bill period when he defined his (and his party's) position between the unyielding policy of the Tories and the excessive demands of the Radicals. This, of course, was a policy of trimming as it was given classic status by George Savile, Marquis of Halifax. However, in 1830–31 Macaulay had not yet adopted this label, nor had he revealed how much he admired, indeed, identified himself with Halifax. This came only in 1838, in his essay on Sir William Temple, and again in his *History of England* (1848, 1855).[47]

When in late 1830 and early 1831 Macaulay turned to French politics of the Restoration period he found exaggerated versions of the same problems that he had identified in England in his own time. He was dealing with a country in which great constitutional changes had been considered – much greater than in England in 1831 – and he recognized that the politicians had been deeply divided, many of them judging the issues in ways that had parallels in English parties and factions.

In France in 1814, as in England, there were ultras who feared anarchy from their ideological opposites, but unlike the ultra-Tories, this fear among the ultras in France was based on their memory of the Revolution. The ultra-royalists wished to retain the institutions, not as they were in 1814, but as they had been before 1789. Although comparatively few in number, their 'hopes . . . began to revive amidst the dangers of the state' (63). Nostalgic for the France of their youth, they were counter-revolutionaries (70). They were not satisfied by the restoration of the institution of monarchy, for they realized that the revolution had been 'a struggle . . . between one caste and another' (70), and that the aristocracy had lost. They were not to be satisfied without a restoration of their property and their old privileges, indeed, their way of life (70, 90). The ultra-royalists were made comparable to the ultra-Tories and to the unyielding defenders of establishments elsewhere, not only by their indifference to liberty, but by their counter-revolutionary posture. The revolutionary dimension of this position was quite real, for, Macaulay argued, the post-revolutionary institutions had gained legitimacy under Napoleon, making it 'impossible to restore the ancient fabric without a second demolition' (69). Thus by 1814, as the Revolution 'was not an innovation, but an establishment,...those who attacked it were the real revolutionists' (74). Just as he had used the label 'fanatic' for the Tories who secretly wished to repeal Catholic emancipation and the Act that provided parliamentary reform, for the royalists he used a synonym – they were zealots (63).[48]

At the other side of the spectrum were the Republicans. Small in number but great in talent and reputation, they felt out of place under the restored monarchy, for they 'hated and feared the Bourbons' (89). Of course they had been even more unhappy with Napoleon, for they had been the victims of his suppression (89). But such was their hatred of royalism and especially of the Bourbons that the prospect of another Napoleonic regime was less offensive to them than Louis's restored monarchy. Consequently they were more than willing to see Louis's new regime subverted.

Macaulay thought the Republicans misjudged the situation. Although they were the 'friends of liberty' (90), by contributing to the subversion of the restored regime, they were facilitating the return of Napoleon from Elba, which would bring war and, in the event of victory, despotism. On the other hand, although they hated the Bourbons, they failed to recognize that under Louis 'the system of society which the revolution has established remained untouched in its essential parts' (90). They should not have been so hostile; there was a free tribune, something of a free press, and peace (90). But 'unhappily, the Republicans consulted their passions rather than their reason' (91), and thus withheld their support, thereby contributing to the incapacity of the regime to resist Napoleon when he returned from Elba. Like some of the extreme Radicals in England, the Republicans ignored the realities while being too identified with and blinded by the 'badges and emblems' of their particular revolutionary tradition.[49] Like the ultra-royalists, they were some-what irrational; they too were 'zealous' (91–92). Thus Macaulay draws our attention to complementary irrationalities in the ultra-royalists and the republicans. The ultras, although professing a concern for stability, in fact were 'enemies . . . of law and order' (73); and the republicans, although professing a concern for liberty, were abetting a return of despotism.

Unfortunately Macaulay did not name the republicans, but he probably had in mind such persons as Lafayette and Carnot. Although he called them the 'friends of liberty' (90), he could not have meant all liberals, for some (e.g. Benjamin

Constant) supported the constitutional monarchy. Indeed, some were the so-called Doctrinaires, with whom he had certain affinities.[50] Nor could he have meant all former supporters of the Revolution, for some had been in the service of Napoleon and some supported Louis's regime. Macaulay acknowledged the small size of the republican group, but as there were so few in it and their beliefs were masked, one may wonder whether Macaulay exaggerated their significance in 1814 as a consequence of projecting backwards from the 1820s (a period he would have been familiar with from the press) when they were visible and important. We may also wonder whether by drawing boundaries round this group, which in 1814 was no more than an unorganized and varied collection of persons with a shared outlook, Macaulay gave a clearer appearance of their reality than the circumstances justified. To this extent he simplified his account of the political struggle to make it compatible with the political themes he wished to emphasize.

There was a third group, the soldiers, that affected the survival of the regime. They were admirers of Napoleon and wished to effect his return. For Napoleon they showed a zeal 'which even the history of religious delusions scarcely furnishes a parallel' (55). Thus, like the ultra-royalists and the republicans, they too were zealots. There was no portion of the community in which antipathy to the Bourbons was so strong, and thus they were ready to take part in the overthrow of the restored monarchy. Indifferent to liberty, they looked forward to Napoleon's return (88–89).

Divided as it was among three extreme, zealous factions, the regime was vulnerable. Each of the groups was willing, some were anxious, to subvert the new government. Whatever was done to conciliate one faction, alienated at least one of the others. Macaulay contrasted France with England at the time he was writing, where, he said, neither of the great parties was revolutionary or counter-revolutionary.[51] On the contrary, instead of opposite principles each represented by separate parties, in England opposing principles were intermixed in all parties and in every individual. This was the source of England's moderation: in 'the great body of the nation, in whose minds, as in their institutions, two hostile principles are blended;' the people love liberty, but their 'love of liberty has a strong tinge of aristocratical feeling' (59). In contrast, in France, where this combination did not exist, the success of either side was unchecked by internal restraint. Thus it was not surprising to Macaulay that at certain times in France the party that had sought liberty created anarchy and those that had sought order created despotism.[52]

Having identified the conflict of extreme factions as the most important and difficult problem in French politics, Macaulay's analysis required that he look for politicians who might have defended the center against the extremes. In the context of English history he had already directed attention to this activity as revealed in the conduct of William III. In his own career, as publicist and politician, he also pointed to this as the most important task for politicians. Also later when he devoted himself to seventeenth-century English history this was emphasized by making Halifax the hero of the Revolution of 1688 and of the *History of England*, thereby giving great prominence to the idea of trimming for which Halifax was the classic spokesman.

In 1830, although he did not use the term, the idea of trimming was in his thoughts, for he cast several French politicians in the role of trimmer and described their conduct in a way that made it congenial to the idea of trimming. His belief in the relevance of this approach for French politics is shown in his identification of Henry IV as 'an example well deserving to be studied and imitated' (74). Henry had conciliated enemies without alienating friends, and he succeeded in unifying a faction-ridden country, and his circumstances were much more difficult than those faced by his descendant (74). Louis XVIII, Macaulay said, "was by no means ill qualified to perform the part of his great ancestor.' He had an excellent understanding and a mild temper; he was without fanaticism; and when the great Revolution began he had shown himself to be a supporter of constitutional restraints on the monarch (75). Macaulay interpreted the Proclamation of St Ouen and the Charter as attempts to balance the opposing demands and fears of the royalists and the republicans (76, 78–81).[53]

Talleyrand was even more clearly cast in the trimmer's role. Like the classic trimmer, he was portrayed as detached and as changing sides without moving to the extremes and as shifting his allegiance only to serve the public interest.

> [He] felt no enthusiastic attachment to the House of Bourbon, [but] saw in the restoration of that house the best means of securing peace with Europe on honourable terms, and of establishing in France a system of government which might unite the blessings of liberty with those of order. . . . it is just to say, that, if he was unfaithful to particular parties and particular families, he was in the main faithful to the interests of his country and to the great principles of government; that, though a revolutionist, he was never a jacobin; and that, though a minister of Napoleon, he had no share in the worst parts of the imperial tyranny (63).

Talleyrand had used his great talents to persuade both the men of the Revolution and the men of the emigration to agree to support the return of Louis XVIII (64), and Macaulay lamented his departure to the Congress of Vienna, for he 'was fitted beyond any man in France, by his talents and his situation, to act the part of mediator between the old dynasty and the new people' (78).[54]

Macaulay seems to have believed that the restored regime could have been successful, despite its vulnerability and despite Napoleon's great appeal; indeed, he believed that it deserved to be supported. In explaining its fall he emphasized internal weaknesses and political failure, and thus did not believe it inevitable that the nation succumb to Napoleon when he returned from Elba. The extreme factions, each for its own reasons wishing to subvert the regime, might have been resisted if popular support for the government had been generated and maintained. Although the Charter did not satisfy the partisans of the emperor or the surviving Jacobins, 'if it had been faithfully observed . . . it would in all probability have satisfied the great body of the nation' (81). But many mistakes were made, and they stimulated suspicion and created grievances: a censorship was proposed which violated the Charter; this violation raised doubts about the guarantees of titles to land purchased from the revolutionary government after confiscation from the Church and the émigrés; the award of honors to those who had adhered to the Bourbons during the Revolution led to a renewal of old class hostilities; and there was discontent about taxes. In addition, old fears associated with the Revolution were allowed to flourish – fear among the peasantry that old feudal privileges were to be re-established; and fear of renewal of religious zeal by the clergy. Also, the government was tarnished by its association in the public mind with the humiliation of invasion and defeat (82–8). Yet, despite these mistakes and misfortunes, 'the great body of the people shrunk from the thought of another revolution' (88). Their reluctance, however, was not sufficient to prevent the overturn, for the attacks by the ultra-royalists and the republicans, combined with the opposition of the soldiers, set the stage for Napoleon's return. Macaulay noted that new governments were easily overthrown (47), and that 'the power of a few zealous men in times of general languor and depression is immense' (63). The hostility of the extreme factions had its intended effect, and Napoleon was allowed his brief success.

Macaulay's *History* ends with Napoleon's return from Elba, Louis's escape, and the battle of Waterloo. Macaulay left no account of the ensuing years to 1830 – of the continuation of Louis's reign, Charles X, and the July Revolution. There is a brief allusion to the Revolution of 1830, but if we were to speculate about how Macaulay might have finished the work, it would be necessary to rely on letters, his essay on Dumont's *Mirabeau* (July 1832), and other scattered comments, and even such evidence is scanty.

The few observations from which one might infer how Macaulay would have evaluated the political developments between 1815 and 1830 are compatible with his view that the 1814 regime was an attempt to break out of the cycle of anarchy and despotism and also with his pessimistic analysis of its prospects. Frenchmen during these years, unlike their ancestors before 1789, did not have to endure the oppressive privileges of a separate caste, and to some small extent they were allowed to discuss political questions and to take part in politics. Thinking of such things, Macaulay in 1832 concluded that the French people had 'lived for seventeen or eighteen years under institutions which, however defective, have yet been far superior to any institutions that had before existed in France.'[55] However, even though an improvement, the regime was not satisfactory, and Macaulay was not disappointed with the changes made in 1830.

Had Macaulay written about the July Revolution he would have approved it, but he would not have approved if it had been excessively violent or destructive. His letters from Paris, written in the immediate aftermath of the July events, reveal a sense of danger more than gratification with the Revolution. He did refer to 'the downfall of the tyrant on the 29th of July,' but he also observed that 'the army is discontented, and that the multitude may become discontented. Such a crisis would be, as you must see, full of danger to property, and might bring back the worst scenes of the former revolution.' With this in mind, it is not surprising that he praised the working people for their moderation and the middle class for serving in the National Guard in order to protect private property and the government against any outbreak of disorder.[56] Nor is it surprising to find that when he wandered about Paris he imagined himself 'in the midst of the French Revolution.'[57]

Welcoming improvement but nervous that the movement promoting it might get out of control, Macaulay approved of change only if it was characterized by moderation both in its methods and its goals. That he regarded the July Revolution as satisfying this criterion is evident in the one allusion to it that appears in the unfinished *History*. Referring to the spirit that broke out in 1789, Macaulay wrote that it 'revived [in 1830] with all its original energy, but with an energy moderated by wisdom and humanity' (62). A similar judgment was made more fully in 1832, soon after he has stopped working on the unfinished history. By noting that Charles X 'violated the fundamental laws of the state [and] established a despotism,' Macaulay was assimilating the July Revolution to the interpretation of England's Glorious Revolution which portrays the revolutionaries as the defenders of the fundamental laws against the despotic king who violated them. And again Macaulay emphasized the moderation of the revolutionaries. In contrast to the first Revolution in France, in 1830 the victors were not vindictive: 'The crime was recent, – the life of the criminal was in the hands of the sufferers . . . [yet] those ministers who has signed the ordinances, . . . were punished only with imprisonment.' Also, in contrast to the first Revolution, property was held sacred, and, in addition, in 1830 one could observe the 'government, in the very moment of triumph and revenge, submitting itself to the authority of a court of law,' and this was proof that 'the law is now stronger than the sword.'[58]

These observations show that, as Macaulay classified revolutions, he placed 1830 with what he termed 'defensive revolutions,' a phrase he actually once used for it. Defensive revolutions were distinguished by the absence of vengeance, hatred, and great destruction and by the presence of some historical continuity; indeed, they were called defensive because their leaders engaged in 'revolutionary' activity in order to defend and preserve some essential features of the polity. In contrast, there were other kinds of revolution in which 'the gulph . . . completely separates the new from the old system.'[59] The consequences of such a revolution horrified Macaulay.

> Revolution [he wrote in 1830] is . . . in itself an evil; – an evil, indeed, which ought sometimes to be incurred for the purpose of averting or removing greater evils, but always an evil. The burden of the proof lies heavy on those who oppose existing governments; nor is it enough for them to show that the government which they purpose to establish is better than that which they purpose to destroy. The difference between two systems must be great, indeed, if it justifies men in substituting the empire of force for that of law; in resolving society back into its original elements; in breaking all those associations which are the safeguards of property and order (71).

Despite his retrospective but qualified defense of the first French Revolution, Macaulay responded to all contemporary revolutionary situations with great caution and usually with alarm.[60]

The defensive revolution was exemplified by 1688. 'The English revolutions,' Macaulay explained, 'have . . . been undertaken for the purpose of defending, correcting, and restoring – never for the mere purpose of destroying.'[61] A defensive revolution was undertaken to protect ancient ways against a ruler such as James II who sought to pervert them. Such a revolution had prescription and legitimacy on its side, and consequently, those who made it had conservative intentions: 'As our Revolution was a vindication of ancient rights, so it was conducted with strict attention to ancient formalities. In almost every word and act may be discerned a profound reverence for the past.'[62] Reflecting this outlook, and expressing a view already made evident when he was writing the unfinished *History of France*, Macaulay decided that 'the only revolutions wh[ich] have turned out well have been defensive revolutions – ours of 1688 – the French of 1830 – the American was, to a great extent, of the same kind.'[63]

We may infer that Macaulay would have concluded his *History of France* on a hopeful note, pointing to the moderation of the revolutionary forces – to their having been defensive in character. Yet we may also wonder about how much conviction this conclusion would have carried. He had already seen how the restored regime in 1814 had failed, and it had also begun as an attempt to make moderation prevail. However, what hopes he might have entertained in 1830 were dashed, for he lived to witness the events of 1848 and 1851, which he interpreted as a return to the cycle of anarchy alternating with despotism. With regard to 1848, he said, everything was confusion and terror; the barricades were streaming with civil blood. He even wondered 'whether the progress of society was not about to be arrested, nay, to be suddenly and violently turned back.' After the revolutionary course was opposed by Napoleon III, Macaulay saw the entire episode in familiar terms. 'Imprudent and obstinate opposition to reasonable demands had brought on anarchy; and as soon as men had a near view of anarchy they fled in terror to crouch at the feet of despotism.'[64]

The situation in France at mid-century presented Macaulay with unattractive alternatives from which, nevertheless, he reluctantly made a choice. He ordered his preferences in the following fashion: 'I am for the President [i.e. Louis Napoleon] against the mountain and for freedom and order against the President, if there be any possibility of having freedom and order in France.'[65] Clearly he thought there was no such possibility, and he decided that avoiding anarchy was less dangerous than the only available alternative.

> I do not like the Emperor or his system. But I cannot find that his enemies are able to hold out any reasonable hope that if he is pulled down, a better govt will be set up. His govt is better than the Red Republic – better probably than that of the military Chief who may take his place – better than civil war.[66]

The situation in France challenged his way of thinking about politics, which assumed that liberty and order could be combined. Throughout his career he had tried to undermine those extremists whose search for order led to a sacrifice of liberty and those whose search for liberty led to a sacrifice of order. But now in France he faced a situation in which one extreme could be defeated only by promoting its opposite. His uneasiness with the choice he made is reflected in his observation on this dilemma:

> Something is to be said for the man who sacrifices liberty to preserve order. Something is to be said for the man who sacrifices order to preserve liberty. For liberty and order are two of the greatest blessings which a society can enjoy; and, when unfortunately they appear to be incompatible, much indulgence is due to those who take either side.[67]

The unfortunate developments in France may have had something to do with Macaulay's failure to complete his *History of France*. He looked on the writing of history as having a political purpose. It was to serve politics by providing politicians

with examples and warnings, and although he often gave warnings, he never neglected the good example. This meant that he identified the kind of institutions that
made moderate politics possible and the attitudes and understandings that sustained
such institutions. This made him look back to examples of politicians who success-
fully led defensive revolutions and who reconciled antagonists and persuaded their
countrymen to agree to timely concessions in order to reduce the influence both of
those whose demands for change and those whose refusals of such demands would
have created antagonism, class conflict, and perhaps civil war. He used the notion
of the 'philosophical historian,' whose role was to identify the best examples of such
wisdom, and he suggested that across great distances of time there was a discernible
connection between the wise statesman whose conduct anticipated the judgment of
posterity and the philosophical historian who perpetuated the memory of such
statesmen and, more important, of their way of thinking and acting. This allowed
the historian to perpetuate a political tradition on which the nation could draw when
it faced, as it inevitably would, new problems and new crises. This would provide
continuity with the past, but of a kind that encouraged flexibility. Such flexibility and
continuity, respectively, represented both radical and conservative intentions, yet
moderated them, so that their manifestations contributed to support the political
center rather than the kind of conflict that led to the alternation of fundamentally
opposed regimes such as Macaulay witnessed in France.

French politics denied Macaulay the opportunity to apply this understanding
of the purpose of history. Despite his favorable judgment of the July Revolution,
he probably sensed the presence of suspicion and class and ideological conflict that
would make it difficult for the regime to survive. Thus when explaining why
Macaulay did not complete his *History of France*, it is sufficient to recall his varied
activities and obligations as Member of Parliament, Edinburgh Reviewer, and
member of the government, but the uncongeniality of the political system in France
to his understanding of his role as historian may also have played a part.

SOURCES

It would be useful to be able to say something about the sources of Macaulay's
information about France. This is difficult, however, for he mentions (50) only one
historian who wrote in part on the same period. This was Mignet, whose *Histoire de
la Révolution Française* was published in 1824. Since Mignet's work extends to 1814,
it could not have influenced what Macaulay wrote about the Restoration, but it did
present a detailed discussion of Napoleon. Mignet condemned Napoleon for
distorting the Revolution and for establishing despotism; but he also admired his

extraordinary achievements, indeed, felt a certain awe for them. Although there is a parallel view in the unfinished *History*, it was not an unusual judgment of Napoleon.[68]

A bibliography of books that Macaulay could have used can be established by examining the books that he is known to have owned and which presumably he read. The best source for this is the shelf list of his library made in 1852 while he was residing at the Albany.[69] The books relevant to his French *History* which were published by 1830–31 when he was writing it can be identified, but of course for most titles there is no way of knowing whether these books were already in his possession in 1830. Another source of information about his library is the Sotheby Catalogue for its sale in March 1863.[70] Since the titles mentioned in the Sotheby Catalogue but not in the shelf list were probably acquired after 1852, its usefulness is reduced; however, it is conceivable that some such titles were inadvertently excluded from the shelf list and that Macaulay owned them when he began work on French history. These sources can be supplemented by his letters, in which he occasionally mentioned books about French affairs.

These sources yield the following titles which Macaulay could have owned before he began writing: Louis Bignon, *Histoire de France, depuis le 18 Brumaire jusqu'à la paix de Tilsitt* (Paris, 1829–38); *Copies of the Original Letters and Despatches of the Generals, Ministers, Grand Officers of State, etc. at Paris, to the Emperor Napoleon at Dresden; intercepted by the advanced Troops of the Allies in the North of Germany* (London, 1814); Lewis Goldsmith, *The Secret History of the Cabinet of Bonaparte* (London, 1810); Barry E. O'Meara, *Napoleon in Exile; or, A Voice from St. Helena* (London, 1822); John Scott, *A Visit to Paris in 1814; being a review of the Moral, Political, Intellectual, and Social Condition of the French Capital* (London, 1815); William Shepherd, *Paris, in eighteen hundred and two, and eighteen hundred and fourteen* (London, 1814); Madame de Staël, *Considérations sur les principaux évenemens de la Révolution Française* (London, 1818); William Warden, *Letters written on board His Majesty's Ship the Northumberland, and at St. Helena* (London, 1816); Helen Maria Williams, *A Narrative of the Events which have taken place in France, from the landing of Napoleon Bonaparte, on the 1st of March, 1815, till the Restoration of Louis XVIII* (London, 1815); and W. T. Williams, *The State of France, 1802–1806* (London, 1807).[71]

Not all these books are of great consequence. Of course they vary in their judgments of Napoleon, and several are critical, but only Bignon's is noteworthy for its extended and on the whole sympathetic defense of Napoleonic policy. Bignon, it should be said, served Napoleon as a diplomat, and his historical work had been commissioned by the Emperor; seven volumes (of eleven) were published by 1830, but the work in the main dealt with military and diplomatic history.[72] The most notable of these books, and the only one to discuss the Restoration regime at considerable length, was Madame de Staël's. Her book, which was first published in

England, where it had considerable influence, is important in the historiography of the Revolution and in the history of Napoleon's reputation, and its part 5, which discussed the first years of the Restoration, could have been a source of influence on Macaulay.[73] There is a considerable array of topics on which there are similar views in her *Considerations* and in Macaulay's unfinished *History*: the analysis of the Charter and especially its preamble; the obstacles to a restoration of pre-revolutionary institutions; the Declaration of St Ouen; the state of public opinion; the assessment of the regime in 1814 as being worthy of allegiance in that it did not violate constitutionally defined rights; and the analysis of the regime as unstable as a result of the strength of factions that sought its downfall. In addition, and perhaps more striking, are observations made by de Staël and Macaulay about the support of both liberty and monarchy by most politicians in England; about the character of Louis XVIII and how Henry IV could have served as a worthy example for him; and the comparison of the restorations of Charles II and Louis XVIII. These parallels are suggestive, but it should be noted that there are disagreements as well, for example, about Talleyrand. Even if Macaulay had read Madame de Staël's book before 1830, since his views in the French *History* reflect an outlook that had its origin in reflections on English history and politics, Madame de Staël should be regarded as having provided confirmation and perhaps some illustration for a view that he developed independently.[74]

Macaulay's personal library also included books that he might have used had he completed his French history, that is, books dealing with the second restoration of Louis XVIII, the reign of Charles X, and the Revolution of 1830. Perhaps the title that would have been most useful was the *Annuaire Historique Universel* by C. L. Lesur. Modelled on the *Annual Register*, this was an annual summary and chronology of events. It began publication with the volume for 1818; Macaulay owned the twelve volumes for the years 1818 through 1829. In addition, he owned *Procès des derniers Ministres de Charles X* (Paris, 1830); Rosignol et Pharaon, *Histoire de la Révolution de 1830* (Paris, 1830).[75]

Even if Macaulay had used all the relevant books in his personal library, they would not have provided all the information included in the unfinished *History*. Unless he disposed of books he used before the shelf list was made, it must be assumed that he supplemented his own modest collection on recent French history by using such libraries as those at the House of Commons and the Athenaeum. It also should be remembered that, as he said of himself, he was 'a very anxious observer of French politics,' and that since he was dealing with recent developments, his dependence on books was somewhat reduced.[76]

Whatever his sources, Macaulay's information about France was integrated with his way of thinking about politics which was well established when he began the

French *History*. Indeed, this work is impressive for its evidence of the imprint of those political and historical themes which were distinctly Macaulay's and which were mainly derived from his reflections about English history and his observations of English politics. It is not that French sources were irrelevant, but in view of the way the analysis of events in France was made to illustrate themes that were ubiquitous in Macaulay's analysis of English history and politics, it may be said that they were comparatively less important as a source. This is not to say that as a general analysis Macaulay's interpretation was incorrect, but that the work has its greatest interest not as French history but for its illumination of Macaulay's way of thinking about politics. Consequently it is not surprising that the work is largely interpretive and contains little plain narrative. One need only consider its main themes to be reminded of Macaulay's other writings. It is the assertion of these themes that gives the unfinished work the stamp of Macaulay's uniqueness, allowing one to say that, even if there were no independent evidence of his authorship, Macaulay certainly wrote it.

NOTES TO INTRODUCTION

1. George Otto Trevelyan, *The Life and Letters of Lord Macaulay* (London, 1876), *1*, 168.
2. Frederick Arnold, *The Public Life of Lord Macaulay* (London, 1862), p. 70.
3. A. N. L. Munby, *Macaulay's Library* (The David Murray Lectures, *28*; Glasgow University Publications, 1966), p. 30.
4. Macaulay to Macvey Napier, 19 August 1830, *The Letters of Thomas Babington Macaulay*, ed. Thomas Pinney (Cambridge University Press, 1974), *1*, 281–2.
5. Brougham to Napier, 8 September 1830, *Selections from the Correspondence of the late Macvey Napier* (London, 1879), p. 88.
6. Macaulay to Napier, 16 October, 17 December 1830, *Letters*, *1*, 309–11, 314. Trevelyan said 'a quarter of a century had not changed Macaulay's estimate of Lord Brougham, nor softened his mode of expressing it. "Strange fellow! His powers gone. His spite immortal. A dead nettle"': Trevelyan, *Life*, *2*, 431. Still smarting in 1842, Macaulay said, 'I should have no scruple in taking a subject out of Brougham's hands': *ibid.*, p. 109.
7. *Ibid.*, *1*, 186–7. For evidence of Brougham's and Macaulay's mutual recriminations see *Napier Correspondence*, pp. 260–3.
8. Macaulay to Napier, 16 October, 16 September 1830: *Letters*, *1*, 299, 309.
9. Dionysius Lardner (1739–1859) was a writer on scientific and technological

subjects and professor of natural philosophy and astronomy at the University of London. He was important as a popularizer of scientific knowledge, both by his own prolific writings, notably on the steam engine, railways, and mathematics, and by means of the 133 volumes of the *Cabinet Cyclopaedia*, which he founded in 1828 and edited. Contributors included Sir Walter Scott, Connop Thirlwall, Thomas Moore, Sir James Mackintosh, Augustus de Morgan, and Sir John Herschel.

10. John Taylor (1781–1864), as the more active partner in the legendary firm of Taylor and Hessey, published, in addition to Clare and Keats, Borrow, Carlyle, De Quincey, Hazlitt, Hood, Lamb, and Landor. He also edited the *London Magazine* (1821–24), was bookseller to the University of London, and wrote on literary, economic, and historical subjects, including two works in which he identified Sir Philip Francis as Junius. See Edmund Blunden, *Keat's Publisher: A Memoir of John Taylor* (London, Jonathan Cape, 1936) and Tim Chilcott, *A Publisher and His Circle* (London, Routledge and Kegan Paul, 1972). Taylor recorded a judgment of Macaulay after hearing him at the Fishmongers' Company dinner, but, alas, he did not refer to the French history. Macaulay's 'appearance was that of a clever mechanic, his manner as little at ease, as abrupt and what the world calls vulgar – using his toothpick for a full hour after Dinner. He spoke like a man of that cast, cleverly, but that was all': John Taylor to James Taylor, 2 November 1833, papers of R. W. P. Cockerton of Bakewell, Derbyshire.

11. Macaulay to Napier, 16 October 1830, *Letters, 1,* 311. Evidently Macaulay also agreed to write biographical works for the *Cabinet Cyclopaedia*, for in an advertisement bound in a copy of a book published in 1833 he was listed as a contributor to 'Eminent British Statesmen' and 'Lives of the Most Eminent Literary and Scientific Men of all Nations'. Both were described as 'works in progress and preparation'. Lardner published such works, but there is no evidence that Macaulay contributed to them.

12. Eyre Evans Crowe was paid £375 for *The History of France* (3 vols.); M. Sismondi received £250 for *A History of the Italian Republics*; Rev. Connop Thirlwall agreed to write *A History of Greece* (5 vols.) for £250. Macaulay may not have received any payment, as typically the contracts provided for payment after publication; Longmans' records for the *Cabinet Cyclopaedia* do not contain an entry indicating that he had been paid.

13. Macaulay's book was called 'a supplement or continuation of [Crowe's] History of France' in an advertisement bound into Mackintosh's *History of England*, vol. 2 (London, 1831). Early advertisements indicated that it was to have been part of the *Cabinet Library* (also edited by Lardner), and only later was

it included in the list of the *Cabinet Cyclopaedia*. Although at one time Crowe's work was advertised as including the period 'to the Deposition of Charles X,' as early as October 1830 Macaulay had undertaken to cover the period 1814 to 1830. Advertisements bound into other volumes of the *Cabinet Cyclopaedia* published in 1830 (Scott, *History of Scotland*, vol. 1 [Philadelphia, 1830]; Crowe, *History of France*, vol. 1 [London, 1830]) gave Macaulay's title as 'The French Revolution of 1830'. Thereafter advertised titles indicated that he was to include the period 1814 to 1830. Advertisements published from 1831 to 1834 also gave Macaulay's title as 'A View of the History of France, From the Restoration of the Bourbons, To the Revolution of 1830'; 'View of the History of France, since the Restoration of the Bourbons'; 'History of France from the Restoration of the Bourbons'.

14. Macaulay to Napier, 16 September 1830, *Letters*, *1*, 298. This explains the exaggerated statement in the *Dictionary of National Biography* that he had written an article on the state of France. Napier had suggested two articles, the one on the events of 1830 to appear first.

15. In a letter of 20 June 1831 Macaulay discussed a passage that appeared at page 63, i.e. on the fourth of the less than six sheets required for the entire fragment. For a discussion of this passage, see note 29 below. On the flyleaf there is a note in an unidentified hand incorrectly stating, 'Set up in type in March 1830'; and the year 1830 appears on the binding, which was made much later. Since the signature-title 'vol. 1' appears on the first leaf of gathering F (pages 65–80), which is the last complete gathering, and since advertisements appearing after June 1831 ceased to describe the work as consisting of two volumes, probably the entire fragment except the proof pages following page 80 was printed by June 1831.

16. Macaulay to Napier, 16 October 1830, 14 March 1831, *Letters*, *1*, 311; *2*, 8. Lord [Henry] Cockburn, *Life of Lord Jeffrey* (Edinburgh, 1852), *2*, 234.

17. Arcole was the name taken by a young man just before he died during the fighting on 28 July 1830 at *la passerelle de Grève*. The bridge was renamed *Pont d'Arcole*. At the time there were many accounts of the incident, e.g. Baron de L[amothe] L[angon], *Une Semaine de l'Histoire de Paris* (Paris, 1830), pp. 240–41; and Percy Sadler, *Paris in July and August 1830; an Historical Narration of the Revolution* (Paris, 1830), p. 147. There was no connection between the subject of this engraving and Arcola, although Napoleon's famous battle on the bridge at Arcola probably inspired the dying words attributed to the hero who took the name Arcole. An engraving portraying the fighting on the bridge at Arcola was commissioned by Longmans for an illustration in Crowe's *History of France*. George Heard Hamilton, 'The Iconographical Origins of Delacroix's "Liberty

Leading the People "'", in *Studies in Art and Literature for Belle da Costa Greene*, ed. D. E. Miner (Princeton University Press, 1954), pp. 61–2, 65; Jacques Hillairet (pseud. for August André Coussillan), *Dictionnaire Historique des Rues de Paris* (Paris, Les Editions de Minuit, 1961), *1*, 106.

18. Miscellaneous Publication Expenses Ledgers, A2, 1820–42, fol. 195, 208; Ledger of Costs and Sales for Lardner's Cabinet Cyclopaedia, 1829–1902, fol. 15, 17: Longman Archives. Corbould's payment of £3–3–0 was entered 10 June 1831. Henry Corbould (1787–1844) was a landscape and miniature painter who did many designs for book illustrations. Edward Francis Finden (1791–1857), an engraver, principally worked on book illustrations. His brother William Finden did the same kind of work. Corbould and Edward Finden collaborated for most of the illustrations in the *Cabinet Cyclopaedia*.

19. An entry dated 31 December 1833 records an expenditure of £9–0–0 to [W.B.] McQueen for printing 6,000 titles for 'Macaulay's France' in October 1831: Ledger of Costs and Sales, fol. 38. The Finden–Corbould illustration was to have been a vignette on the title page. McQueen's specialized in printing illustrations: see Iain Bain, 'Thomas Ross & Son. Copper- and Steel-plate Printers since 1833,' *Journal of the Printing Historical Society*, no. 6, 1966, p. 13. Following an entry showing £3–3–0 paid to Corbould for the drawing there is the comment 'Not Used' (Miscellaneous Publication Expenses Ledger, fol. 208). However, since Finden was paid for the engraving, and as McQueen appears to have been paid to produce title pages, one may conclude that the illustrated title pages were produced, and that they were 'not used' in the sense of not having been used as part of a published volume. None have been found, and a search for Finden's engraving has been unsuccessful.

20. Ledger of Costs and Sales, fol. 16; Miscellaneous Publication Expenses Ledger, fol. 208. The copyist was paid £1–17–6.

21. Tardner's expectations for the completion of Macaulay's book are approximately indicated by the advertisements bound into some of the other volumes of the *Cabinet Cyclopaedia* that were published from 1831 to 1834. In 1831, the book was described as a 'forthcoming volume' and it was announced for publication on 1st April, 2nd May, 1st June, and 1st November. In 1832 it was advertised as 'nearly ready,' and it was listed with 'Volumes for Early Publication.' In 1833 it was placed with 'Volumes in Immediate Preparation.' See also *Letters*, 1, 324 (appx.).

22. Macaulay to Napier, 29 October 1831. In a letter of 14 March 1831 he anticipated 'completing the first volume': *Letters*, 2, 8, 107. The signature–title 'vol. 1' appears on the first leaf of gatherings B, D, E, and F. However, advertisements printed after June 1831 either stated that Macaulay's book would be complete in one volume or they did not specify the number of volumes.

23. Trevelyan, not unreasonably, described the printed pages as being 88 in number, for the last page was numbered 88. However, these numerals are in ink, and they replaced the numeral 9, which was deleted; and there is a hiatus between page 87 and the page that was incorrectly numbered 88. Furthermore, this could not have been page 88, for it was printed as a recto and therefore as an odd-numbered page, with the printed numeral 9 appearing above the right margin, as it did on all the other recto pages. (On even-numbered pages the numerals appear above the left margin.) Evidently the type for one of the numerals dropped, leaving the numeral 9. The page could have been, say, 91 or perhaps 93, for the printed numeral 9 is not flush with the right margin, as it was on almost all the other recto pages, suggesting that it was the first of a two-digit numeral, such as 91. On the other hand, the numerals for page 87 also are not flush with the margin.

24. Trevelyan, *Life*, *1*, 168.

25. There are many indications that the pages following 80 were proofs. They contain many errors corrected in ink, though evidently not in Macaulay's hand. The leaf following page 80 appears to have been a wrapper for what followed (i.e. pp. 81–9, of which pages 81 and 88 are missing). This leaf is blank and soiled, and in addition to the note indicating that the type had been distributed, it contains, in G. A. Spottiswoode's hand, the note, 'Fragment by Macaulay – Never published'. This suggests that pages 81–9 were physically separate from pages 1–80 before being combined with the first eighty pages. These later pages are disjunct leaves, placed in normal page order, with the appropriate recto or verso pages blank. Finally, there is a note in the tail margin of page 80 saying that '8 pages beyond this not imposed' (i.e. corrected and imposed for printing).'

26. Macaulay to Napier, 19 December [1831]; Macaulay to Hannah and Margaret Macaulay, 19 June [1832], *Letters, 2,* 108, 134.

27. Macaulay to Napier, 17 December 1830, *ibid., 1,* 314.

28. 'Civil Disabilities of the Jews' (January 1831); 'Sadler's *Refutation,* refuted' (January 1831); 'Moore's *Life of Lord Byron*' (June 1831); 'Croker's edition of Boswell's *Life of Johnson*' (September 1831); 'Southey's edition of the *Pilgrim's Progress*' (December 1831).

29. 'Your criticism is to a certain [extent?] just – But you have not considered the whole sentence together. *Depressed* is in itself better than *weighed down*. But "the *oppressive* privileges which had *depressed* industry" would be a horrible cacophony': Macaulay to Hannah Macaulay, 20 June 1831, *Letters, 2,* 48. In the fragment the passage was changed to read, 'oppressive privileges which anciently depressed industry' (page 63, where there are no corrections). In

the same letter Macaulay reported having corrected an earlier passage, but there are no manuscript corrections in the earlier part of the fragment.

30. That these particular pages are missing can be explained by their accessibility to the printing house employee as he began distribution. With regard to pages 17–80, that is, gatherings C, D, E, and F, where parts of pages are missing, it is the bottom parts; and the missing page (p. 35) could well have been at the bottom of the forme. With regard to what would have been the first gathering, eight of the missing pages (2, 3, 6, 7, 10, 11, 14, 15) would have been together within one forme; and the other four missing pages (4, 5, 12, 13) would have been together on one-half of a forme. Pages 81 and 88, which as part of proof copy were single leaves, probably are missing because they were separated from the other pages of proof copy before the surviving pages of proof were combined with pages 1–80. There is a note on the flyleaf, initialled 'N': 'Nothing more remains.'

31. There would have been one variation on this procedure. Since most of the type for the first gathering had been distributed before the presumed rescue occurred, it must be assumed that the rescuer, on finding only pages 1, 8, 9, 16 for the first sheet intact, pulled pages 1 and 16, which are next to one another on an octavo sheet, and then used the blank side of the same paper to pull pages 8 and 9, thus making page 8 the verso of page 1 and page 16 the verso of page 9. And apparently he twice pulled sheets for pages 65–80, for unbound they exist in duplicate. The rescue hypothesis is supported by the observation made by G. A. Spottiswoode that 'none was worked off'; and it is compatible with his report of an entry in a work book indicating that the firm had composed 56 pages of Macaulay's book. Of course this entry was incomplete. G. A. Spottiswoode to Thomas Norton Longman, 5 May 1898, Longman Archives.

32. Note dated 5 October 1860, Longman Archives. (The note is dated 10/5/60. Because Spottiswoode in other letters placed the month before the day, I have rendered this as 5 October 1860 and not as 10 May.) Trevelyan, *Life*, *1*, 168. On the flyleaf there is the note in the hand of Thomas Longman IV, 'This fragment of Macaulay's History of France was found in Spottiswoode's printing office, 10/5/60.' This information was evidently copied from the G. A. Spottiswoode note.

33. On 16 April 1851 the *Cabinet Cyclopaedia*, including stock and copyrights, was sold for £9,500. The Longman firm, which previously owned a one-third interest in it, was the purchaser. Taylor told Longman 'What a valuable property the copyright of Mackintosh's [History of] England would be to them if they got Macaulay to connect his History with it. No doubt this had occurred to them before': John Taylor to James Taylor, 24 May 1850, Taylor of Bakewell Papers,

Derbyshire County Record Office, Matlock. Macaulay's *History of England*, volumes 1 and 2, were published by Longmans late in 1848; Mackintosh's narrative in his *History*, which was part of the *Cabinet Cyclopaedia*, terminated with 1536.

34. *Speeches of the Right Honourable T. B. Macaulay* (London, 1854), pp. 34 (5 July 1831), 80 (16 December 1831).

35. *Ibid.*, p. 77 (16 December 1831); 'On Mitford's History of Greece' (November 1824), *Miscellaneous Writings of Lord Macaulay* (London, 1860), *1*, 176.

36. By locating Charles's oppression in the ecclesiastical realm, this judgment is much less critical of Charles's reign than others that Macaulay made; compare 'Milton', *Edinburgh Review*, *42* (August 1825), 328 and *History of England*, ed. C. H. Firth (London, 1913), *1*, 77–8. However, even when compared with these and other portrayals of the Stuarts, Napoleon still exemplifies a more pure form of despotism. Macaulay also compared Napoleon with Cromwell, who 'was less absolute than Napoleon' (45); also see 'Hallam,' *Edin. Rev. 48* (September 1828), 141–6.

37. 'Essay on the Life and Character of King William III' (1822), ed. A. N. L. Munby, *Times Literary Supplement*, 1 May 1969, pp. 468–9.

38. 'A Conversation between Mr. Abraham Cowley and Mr. John Milton, touching the Great Civil War' (1824), *Misc. Wr.*, *1*, 121.

39. 'Essay on William III,' p. 469.

40. For example, see *History of England*, *4*, 1828–29.

41. Perhaps it is worth repeating Macaulay's comment at age thirteen: 'I cannot conceive a greater punishment to Buonaparte than that which the allies have inflicted upon [him]. How can his ambitious mind support it? All his great projects and schemes which once made every throne in Europe tremble, are buried in the solitude of an Italian isle': Macaulay to his mother, 11 April 1814, *Letters*, *1*, 42.

42. 'Hallam,' *Edin. Rev.*, *48* (September 1828), 169; 'Walpole's *Letters to Sir Horace Mann*,' *ibid.*, *58* (October 1833), 234.

43. *Speeches*, pp. 18 (2 March 1831), 28–9, 31 (5 July 1831), 54 (10 October 1831).

44. 'Southey's *Colloquies on Society*,' *Edin. Rev.*, *50* (January 1830), 533.

45. *Speeches*, p. 33 (5 July 1831).

46. *Ibid.*, p. 76 (16 December 1831).

47. 'The life and writings of Sir William Temple,' *Edin. Rev.*, *68* (October 1838), 169–70. *History of England*, *1*, 234; *3*, 1168–9, 1328.

48. *Hansard's Parliamentary Debates*, 3rd series, *51*, 827, 830 (29 January 1840).

49. Charles Lord Spencer exemplified a corrupt and degenerate Whigism that was

akin to radicalism; like certain Latin poets and orators, he 'meant by liberty something very different from the only liberty which is of importance to the happiness of mankind. Like them, he could see no danger to liberty except from kings': *History of England, 6*, 2734. See also pp. 91–92 below.

50. On these affinities, see Vincent E. Starzinger, *Middlingness.* JUSTE MILIEU *Political Theory in France and England, 1815–48* (Charlottesville, University Press of Virginia, 1965).

51. *Speeches*, p. 24 (5 July 1831).

52. 'In most other countries there is no middle course between absolute submission and open rebellion': 'Mirabeau,' *Edin. Rev., 55* (July 1832), 564.

53. In a brief discussion of Louis's policy at the beginning of the second restoration, Macaulay described Louis as trying to be conciliatory, and as deviating from this policy only because of great pressure. The ultras dominated the new Chamber and threatened 'a new Reign of Terror' of their own. 'The government was not disposed to treat even the regicides with severity,' and therefore the king and his ministers 'exerted themselves to restrain the violence of the fanatical royalists.' However, 'it was thought necessary to make some concession,' and it was decided to exile those who had voted for the death of Louis XVI and those who had supported Napoleon during the hundred days. But this was lenient, Macaulay said, when compared with what the ultras demanded, 'Barère's *Memoirs*,' *Edin. Rev., 79* (April 1844), 345.

54. Macaulay met Talleyrand soon after he wrote these passages: Macaulay to Hannah Macaulay, 11 July 1831, *Letters, 2*, 67–8. See also Macaulay's observations on Lainé and Constant (61–62, 96–97).

55. 'Mirabeau,' *Edin. Rev., 55* (July 1832), 562. For a less complacent view of French politics under the Restoration, see his letter of 5 October 1822 to his father. 'I am impatient for what, I fear, can alone terminate this [the slave trade] and innumerable other abuses, an explosion in France, which may at once overthrow a family on which prosperity and adversity, empire and exile, have in vain been tried': *Letters, 1*, 179. Although this statement may have been provoked by the resurgence of the Right, it also should be interpreted in light of the fact that Macaulay knew that his father found slavery and revolution equally abhorrent.

56. Journal Letter, [21–22 September 1830], *ibid., 1*, 305. Approval of French developments was not unusual in England; for example, see Henry Brougham, 'The late Revolution in France,' *Edin. Rev. 52* (October 1830), 1–25. The analogy between 1830 and 1688 'became a stock theme in the national press': N. Gash, 'English Reform and French Revolution in the General Election of

1830,' in *Essays presented to Sir Lewis Namier*, ed. R. Pares and A. J. P. Taylor (London, Macmillan, 1956), p. 269.

57. Trevelyan, *Life*, *1*, 183.

58. 'Mirabeau,' *Edin. Rev.*, *55*, 561–2. Although in 1832 he was impressed by the way the wish for revenge had been restrained, when he was in Paris in September 1830 Macaulay thought there was a risk of rebellion if the wish for revenge against Polignac and Peyronnet was not to be gratified: Journal Letter, [21–22 September 1830], *Letters*, *1*, 305. A few years later he was quite condescending towards Niebuhr for having been alarmist about the Revolution of 1830: Macaulay to Ellis, 29 May 1835, in *Letters*, *3*, 143.

59. *History of England*, *1*, 22.

60. For a rare exception, see note 55 above. The passages quoted, as well as others in the unfinished History (71, 73), indicate that Macaulay did not approve of the French Revolution that began in 1789 and that he thought those who at the time supported it were without justification. Elsewhere his recognition of the evils accompanying the Revolution was greatly qualified by his belief in the value of its long-term benefits. 'The evil was temporary, and the good durable': 'Mirabeau,' *Edin. Rev.*, *55*, 557; also see 558–61. The Revolution, 'in spite of all its crimes and follies, was a great blessing to mankind'; 'Sir James Mackintosh's *History of the Revolution*,' *ibid.*, *61* (July 1835), 276. These mixed and qualified judgments are almost entirely absent in the unfinished History.

61. 'Mirabeau,' *loc. cit.*, *55*, 572.

62. *History of England*, *3*, 1310.

63. Journals, vol. 11, fol. 409 (29th December [1858]), in Trinity College Library, Cambridge. He associated 1830 with 1688 in 'Barère,' *Edin. Rev.*, *79* (April 1844), 293. Of course the idea of a defensive revolution recalls Burke's similar phraseology and his distinguishing the revolutions of which he approved from the French Revolution. *The Works of the Right Honourable Edmund Burke* (London, 1887), *3*, 225; *4*, 80.

64. *Speeches*, pp. 505–6 (2 November 1852). When in November 1848 he was writing a part of his *History* that celebrated the revolution of 1688, he contrasted that event with the revolutions of 1848 in France and elsewhere: *History of England*, *3*, 1310–12. And in his diary he wrote, 'What good have the revolutions of 1848 done? Or rather what harm have they not done? Here is France worse than in 1788 after seventy years of revolutions': Journals, vol. 11, fol. 409 (29 December [1858]).

65. Journals, vol. 4, fol. 321 (4 December [1851]). He also wrote, 'The coup d'etat struck. . . . I never cared so little about a revolution. Things were so bad that nothing could well make them worse as respects France' (2 December

[1851]); and, 'What a strange business this is in France. Yet I am not disposed to think ill of it. Here it w[oul]d be insupportable that the army sh[oul]d overrule the civil power. But there – what is there steady or well-organized or deserving of trust but the army? Whatever is not army is chaos. The soldier in France now is what the priest was in Europe six centuries ago – he must govern, and ought to govern' (3 December [1851]): Journals, vol. 4, fol. 319–20.

66. Journals, vol. 11, fol. 323–4 (28 May [1858]). He added, '[the French] are incapable of being well governed – that a people which violently pulls down constitutional governments and lives quiet [sic] under despotism, must be and ought to be despotically governed. We should have reformed the gov[ernmen]t of the H[ouse] of Orleans without subverting it. We should not have borne the yoke of celui-ci for one day.'

67. *History of England, 4*, 1711.

68. Already in 1822 Macaulay called Napoleon one of 'the great mixed Characters of ancient and modern times,' like Alexander, Caesar, Peter, Cromwell, and Elizabeth. He acknowledged that Napoleon, like most princes, had massacred and oppressed; but he also recognized that Napoleon had eliminated ancient abuses and had established an admirable system of jurisprudence. Macaulay traced this judgment to Barry O'Meara's *Napoleon in Exile [or, A Voice from St. Helena; the Opinions and Reflections of Napoleon on the most Important Events of his Life and Government in his own words* (London, 1822)], a book, Macaulay said, which 'has made me Buonapartiste . . . [that is,] comparatively, with reference to my former opinions of the man': Macaulay to Zachary Macaulay, 5 October 1822, *Letters, 1*, 180.

69. 'Library of the Right Honble. T. B. Macaulay. November 1852. List of Books,' at Wallington.

70. *Catalogue of A Portion of the Interesting and Valuable Library of the late Right Honble. Lord Macaulay . . . which will be sold by auction . . . 4th March, 1863.*

71. These titles are from the shelf list, except W. T. Williams, *State of France*, which is item 834 in the Sotheby Catalogue; Shepherd, *Paris*, which was mentioned in a letter dated 26 August 1830; and O'Meara, *Napoleon in Exile*, which was mentioned in a letter (see note 68 above). The shelf list usually provides abbreviated titles without dates. Although some books were published in more than one edition, I have given dates of the first editions.

72. Pieter Geyl, *Napoleon For and Against* (New Haven, 1948), pp. 37–44.

73. *Ibid.,* pp. 19–22. Hedva Ben-Israel, *English Historians on the French Revolution* (Cambridge University Press, 1968), p. 50. Stanley Mellon, *The Political Uses of History; A Study of Historians in the French Restoration* (Stanford University Press, 1958), pp. 7–9.

74. Macaulay met Madame de Staël's son, Baron Auguste de Staël, in 1822; in 1830 he visited her daughter and son-in-law, Victor, duc de Broglie. About her *De l'Allemagne* (1813), Macaulay said, 'The book is a foolish one in some respects – but it abounds with information and shews great mental power.' And he added, 'She was certainly the first [wom]an of her age – Miss Edgeworth, I think, the second, and Miss Austen the third' (1831): *Letters, 1,* 176, 300: *2,* 84.

75. The *Annuaire Historique Universel*, the *Procès*, and the *Histoire* by Rossignol and Pharaon are listed in the Sotheby catalogue (items 35, 390, and 405, respectively). The *Annuaire Historique Universel* is in the shelf list. Of course, his library also included books that were relevant to his French History, but which had not been published when he wrote it: for example, Jean Capefigue, *Histoire de la restauration et des causes qui ont amené la chute de la branche ainée des Bourbons* (Paris, 1831–33, 10 vols.), which is in the shelf list.

76. Macaulay to Napier, 16 October 1830, *Letters, 1,* 309.

BIBLIOGRAPHICAL NOTE

'The History of France, from the Restoration of the Bourbons to the Accession of Louis Philippe.' This title appears on p. [1]. There is no preliminary matter.

The pages, numbered up to [8]9 [i.e. 88], were set 39 lines to the page and were imposed for proofing in octavo as gatherings signed B–G and paged [1], 8, 9, 16–34, 36–80, 82–87, [8]9 [i.e. 88]. (Pages 2–7, 10–15, 35, 81 and 88 do not appear.) Page 19 has only the first 11 lines, page 20 only the first 33 lines, and page [8]9 [i.e. 88] only the first 24 lines, the type for the remainder of these pages having been distributed. There are printed running titles ('History of France' or 'The History of France') on the versos of all leaves except the last which has the running title in manuscript. 'Vol. I' appears as part of the signature on B_1r, D_1r, E_1r, and F_1r. There are many dropped letters, especially at the ends of words appearing at the outer margins and in the top and bottom lines. On pp. 82–8[9] there are many compositional errors which are corrected in ink.

The detailed collation is as follows:

B_1: recto, p. [1]; verso, p. 8
[B_5]: recto, p. 9; verso, p. 16
C_1–C_8: pp. [17]–32
D_1: pp. 33–34
D_2: recto, blank; verso, p. 36
D_3–D_8: pp. 37–48
E_1–E_8: pp. 49–64
F_1–F_8: pp. 65–80
[G_1]: blank on both sides (except for handwritten comments described hereafter)
G_2: recto, blank; verso, p. 82
G_3: recto, p. 83; verso, blank
G_4: recto, blank; verso, p. 84
G_5: recto, p. 85; verso, blank
G_6: recto, blank; verso, p. 86
G_7: recto, p. 87; verso, blank
G_8: recto, blank; verso, p. 9 [i.e. 89?] ('9' deleted, '88' inserted by hand)

The volume is bound in brown tooled leather, and in gold lettering it is identified as 'Fragments of a History of France by Thomas Babington Macaulay. 1830.' There are marbled end papers. Preceding page [1] there are 9 binder's leaves, all blank except the first, which serves as a flyleaf. Page [89] is followed by 9 blank binder's leaves.

There are the following handwritten comments (in addition to the many corrections on pp. 82–[89]):

On the flyleaf: '*Thomas Longman. Pater Noster Row. This fragment of Macaulays History of France was found in Spottiswoode's printing office./10/5/60.*' [in Thomas Longman's hand] '*Set up in type in March 1830.*' [in an unidentified hand]. '*Nothing more remains.N.*' [in an unidentified hand]

In the head margin of p. [1]: '*Distributed. (greater part before it was pulled.)*' [in an unidentified hand].

In the head margin of p. [17]: '*Distributed. (19 and 20 in part before being pulled).*' [in an unidentified hand]

In the head margin of p. 33: '*Distributed*' [in an unidentified hand]

In the head margin of p. 49: '*distributed*' [in an unidentified hand]

In the head margin of p. 65: '*Distributed*' [in an unidentified hand]

In the tail margin of p. 80: '*8 pages beyond this not imposed*' [in an unidentified hand]

On top of soiled, blank leaf following p. 80: '*Distributed*' [in an unidentified hand]; '*Fragment by Macaulay – Never published*' [in George Andrew Spottiswoode's hand].

The text is reproduced, except for the following alterations. Mis-spelled words have been corrected where the mis-spelling was caused by dropped letters, and then only if there can be no doubt about the word that was intended. The spellings of a few proper names have been corrected (Barère, Bastille, Billaud-Varenne, Fontainebleau, Guadet, Lanjuinais, Montesquiou and Napoleon). Full words that have been editorially provided are placed within brackets. Missing punctuation has been supplied where the gap was caused by dropped punctuation marks, and cases of faulty punctuation, which obviously were caused by errors in composition, have been corrected. In one case a repeated word has been deleted. Running titles, signatures, and signature titles have not been reprinted.

There is a table on page 117 that gives the page and line numbers in the present edition of the first lines of each page in the corresponding text as printed in the copy in the archives of Longman Group Ltd.

NAPOLEON AND THE
RESTORATION OF THE BOURBONS

from

*The History of France from the Restoration of the Bourbons
to the Accession of Louis Philippe*

HISTORY OF FRANCE

There are two portions of modern history pre-eminently important and interesting – the history of England from the meeting of the long parliament to the second expulsion of the Stuarts; and the history of France from the opening of the states-general at Versailles to the accession of the house of Orleans. It is not too much to say, that neither of these portions of history will ever be thoroughly comprehended by any man who has not often looked at them in connexion, and carefully examined the numerous points of analogy and of contrast which they present.

The revolution which took place in England during the seventeenth century produced no immediate effect on the institutions of foreign countries. Neither our situation nor our national character qualified us to promulgate our political creed. The people of the continental monarchies were not, in the days of Louis the Fourteenth, sufficiently enlightened to receive it. We were separated from our neighbours by our geographical position. We were separated from them still more by

[six pages missing]

against them. Charles the First had solemnly promised to redress them.

Thus the great body of those who opposed the Stuarts had in view no other object than the securing of the legitimate institutions of England. Having constantly in their minds a well-known and domestic pattern, they paid little attention to abstract reasoning, or to the ex-

43

amples of other times and other countries. It is remarkable, that though ancient literature was regarded with far greater veneration in the time of Charles the First than during the last century, the leaders of the popular party in the time of Charles the First did not borrow a single ceremony or title from Greece or Rome. No classical allusion, no general theory of politics, affected them so much as their own old and familiar words, magna charta, habeas corpus, trial by jury, privilege of parliament. They never took the trouble to enquire whether liberty was the inalienable right of men; they were content to know that it was the lawful birthright of Englishmen. Their social contract was no fiction. It was still extant on the original parchment, sealed with the wax which had been affixed at Runnymede, and attested by the noble names of the Mariscals and Fitzherberts. Thus our ancestors carried into rebellion the feeling of legitimacy; and, even in the act of innovating, appealed to ancient prescription. In the wildest license of faction and civil war, they still preserved something of the gravity which belongs to ancient and firmly established governments. The Royalists were overcome by the Presbyterians; but we had nothing like the massacres of September. The Presbyterians were overcome by the Independents; but we had nothing like the vengeance inflicted by the Mountain on the Gironde. Extraordinary judicatures were established in England; but the revolutionary tribunal of Paris often sent to the scaffold in one day five times as many victims as were condemned after our civil war by all the high courts of justice. The English nobles were at the most violent crisis of the civil dissensions, deprived of their political power by the soldiers; but the nation looked on that proceeding with disgust. The peers retained their property, their titles, and a large share of public respect. Ceremonious honours were paid to them by the revolutionary government; and they at length resumed their political functions with the general approbation of the people. The same venerable institutions which had curbed the monarchy, curbed also the revolution which overthrew the monarchy, and the military sovereignty which succeeded to the revolution. The same spirit which had saved the five members from the vengeance of the king saved Lilburn from the vengeance of the commonwealth, and Mordaunt from the vengeance of the protector. Cromwell found himself thwarted in all his arbitrary projects by parliaments and juries. He was less absolute than Napoleon, because the English republicans had been less violent than the Jacobins; and the English republicans were less violent than the Jacobins, because the government of the Stuarts had been milder than that of the Bourbons. The recoil was moderate, because the compression had been moderate.

The government of Charles the First, though in many things unconstitutional, had in one point only been cruelly oppressive; and it is remarkable that precisely on that point the strongest re-action took place. The worst part of the system which preceded the civil war was the restraint imposed on religious opinions. The worst excesses of the popular party, – indeed, all their excesses, – were produced by the intemperance of religious zeal. It has often been observed, that there is a striking contrast between the theological extravagance of the Puritans and their wisdom in political matters. The explanation is simple. The violence of the rebound was proportioned to the violence of the original movement. In spite of the illegal proceedings of the Stuarts, the civil government had been in the main good. The ecclesiastical government had been intolerable. Our ancestors, therefore, came soberly and with self-command

[six pages missing]

tyranny of the capital, and the representative assembly from the tyranny of its own galleries. The ends were honourable, and the means seemed fully adequate to the ends. To this party the majority of the convention was attached. To this party the departments oppressed by Paris, and the higher classes of Paris oppressed by the multitude, looked for protection. To this party belonged the most distinguished orators, philosophers, and soldiers of the republic, – Brissot, Vergniaud, Lanjuinais, Guadet, Condorcet, Dumourier. The fate of this celebrated political connexion is full of matter for solemn and melancholy thought. They attempted to arrest the work of destruction; and they perished almost without a struggle. The most eloquent public men of France were dragged from the tribune before the faces of their terrified colleagues. The general, who had arrested the march of the foreign invaders, was compelled to take refuge in the hostile camp. The errors

45

of the Girondists, both speculative and practical, were indeed great: but some of them will always have honourable mention from impartial historians, as men who, being free to choose between death and crime, advisedly and with open eyes, resolved to suffer cruelty rather than to inflict it.

When the royalists, the constitutionalists, and the Girondists had been successively beaten down, a new and more formidable opponent arose. The bravest and fiercest of those who had hitherto seemed to lead the movement attempted to check it. Danton, strong in his talents, in the force of his character, and in the recollection of bloody services unshrinkingly performed, wished to put an end to those excesses, of which he had afforded the first and the most dreadful example. No man had given dearer pledges to the revolution; no man was surrounded by firmer or more zealous partisans; but it was in vain. All-powerful to exterminate, he was impotent to save. The author of the reign of terror, the captain of the ruffians of September, died the martyr of mercy and order.

The day of the downfall of Robespierre marks [the] point at which the great impulse of the revolution ceased. Considered in itself, indeed, that event was merely [a] victory gained by a few wicked and desperate men over their accomplices. Robespierre and Couthon were assuredly not more odious than Collot d'Herbois and Billaud-Varenne; and compared with Barère de Vieussac, St Just almost inspires respect. But the memorable 9th of Thermidor had all the characteristics of a turning point. It was the first day since 1789 on which those who wished to stop the progress of the revolution had gained a decisive advantage over those who wished to propel it. It was the first day on which those in whose minds the jacobinical fanaticism which had began to languish had shown themselves stronger than those over whom it still retained undiminished power. After five years, during which a succession of insurrections had put down a succession of established governments, an established government had, with signal promptitude and vigour, put down an insurrection. The energy had passed from the aggressive to the defensive side. The fury of the revolution had spent itself. The work of destruction was done. The old society had passed away, and the new creation commenced.

46

In all communities in which large armies exist, the tendency of things, after great and violent revolutions, is always towards military despotism; and the reason is plain. The obedience which societies pay to constituted authorities is rather the effect of habit and association, than of reason. A government which has stood for ages, and which we have been, from our childhood upwards, accustomed to obey, necessarily acquires a certain sacredness in our eyes. We naturally shrink from the thought of resisting authority which has scarcely ever within the memory of man, been resisted, and which has never been resisted with success. The idea of rebellion is connected in our minds with the idea of ignominy and guilt. These feelings constitute the strength of governments; and these feelings a government which has sprung from the convulsions of a destructive revolution, and which is new in all its principles and forms, cannot inspire. It can plead no prescription. It is fenced by no feeling of habitual veneration, such as that which made Cæsar pause on the banks of the Rubicon; such as that which induced Ebroin and Pepin to exercise their sovereign power under the names of imbecile and secluded princes; such as that which, in the great contest between the English and the Mahrattas for the empire of India, made each party so desirous to have in its power the blind and decrepit heir of Tamerlane. A polity recently established has no such hold on the public mind. Its own principle is that rebellion may be justifiable. Its own existence proves that rebellion may be successful. The obedience which we pay to such a government is matter not of feeling, but of pure calculation. No man entertains towards it any sentiment of loyalty. No man is shocked at the thought of rising up against it. If it falls, no man misses it.

Nothing is harder than to overturn an old government, and nothing easier than to overturn a new one. Our own history affords some remarkable proofs of these propositions. It took twenty years of discontent and parliamentary opposition, and four years of civil war, to pull down the Stuarts. But the long parliament was scattered by a word; and Richard Cromwell fell without a blow. It is on this account that politic statesmen have always been desirous to disguise innovations as much as possible under ancient names and badges. Where this is judiciously done, institutions which are in fact new may speedily acquire all the authority of age. If Cromwell had taken the title of king, held chapters of the garter, and created his son prince of Wales, the crown might still have remained in his family. If our first magistrate had, in 1689, been styled protector of the commonwealth of England, though the distribution of power in the state had been exactly such as it now is, the Stuarts would probably have been a second time restored. At Rome, the chief who openly trampled on the constitution died by violence: his more cautious heir, who introduced despotism under the forms of the constitution, died of old age.

When the public mind is in that fluctuating and agitated state in which a deep and searching revolution leaves it, – when rulers are rising and falling day by day, – when fundamental laws are as transitory as the fashions of apparel, – one thing is stable in the midst of instability, and vigorous in the midst of weakness. In one

[28 lines missing]

[con]stitutional proceedings, a general disposition to bear with many evils and abuses rather than violate fixed and known rules of law. Of this there was nothing in France during the four years which preceded the military usurpation. It was not, indeed, a time of violent passions or atrocious crimes: but there was nothing certain in the state. The constitution existed only on paper. The disputes of the hostile parties were decided by those violent means which it is the very end and aim of government to render unnecessary. There was no law but strength; and the strength was with the army.

Every circumstance favoured the ambition of the military adventurer who stood at the head of the soldiers of France. His great victories had not, like those of Cromwell, been gained over his own countrymen. His glory belonged to no party, but was the common property of the whole nation. The royalists preferred his rule to a democracy. The jacobins preferred it to a restoration. The great body of the people, sick of incessant change, and detesting alike the memory of the old monarchy and of the reign of terror, welcomed with delight a chief who announced himself as the champion at once of the revolution and of social order. Those political theories, which had dazzled the subjects of Louis the Sixteenth, had lost almost all their influence. A cruel

48

experience had taught France that something more than a specious theory of natural rights is necessary to make a good government. The philanthropists had reigned, and their tender mercies had been cruel. The philosophers had reigned, and the extravagance of their fanaticism had surpassed that of the wildest religious mystics. Ardent professions of benevolence and public spirit had

[6 lines missing]

degree all those intellectual qualities which distinguish the founders of dynasties from their successors. His moral character, on the other hand, was such as is rarely found, except in princes born to despotic power. With talents for war and government not inferior to those of Julius Cæsar, he united a violence of temper and an impatience of all opposition, such as the Greek historians ascribe to Cambyses and Xerxes. The insult offered by Cambyses to the Egyptian god was not more indecent or impolitic than the conduct of Bonaparte towards the pope; and the chaining of the Hellespont was at least as wise a measure as the decrees of Berlin and Milan. Several circumstances are reported on undeniable authority, which, though trifling in themselves, mark the character of the man on whom the destiny of France so long depended. During the campaign of 1813, a gust of wind disarranged the map which he was consulting; he dashed it to the ground in a paroxysm of rage. On another occasion, a dog barked at the heels of his horse; he drew his pistol, and fired at the animal which annoyed him: the shot missed, and he flung the pistol away. We may laugh at a spoiled child who beats the ground on which it has fallen; but in the leader of six hundred thousand soldiers, and the sovereign of fifty millions of subjects, such bursts of senseless fury are matter for any thing but laughter.

It is not easy to understand how a man of very great talents, who had been born in an obscure rank, who had been educated under a rigid discipline, who had passed through the lower grades of military service, who had known poverty and dependence, who had married from attachment, who was happy in domestic life, and who retained to the last many of the tastes and feelings of the class from which he sprang, should have been selfish, arbitrary, capricious, and intolerant of restraint to a degree very unusual even in despots surrounded by flat-

terers, from the cradle taught to believe that every thing is made for
them, and accustomed to find every thing bend to them. Yet thus it was.
To be absolute, to be alone in power without equal or second, to
experience no resistance or delay in any quarter, seemed to be as
necessary as the breath of life to a man who, a few years before his
elevation, had lodged in a garret, and dined at a low eating-house.

The form of government which he established was worthy of powers
so great and so perverted. There is in his political institutions a kind of
reversed providence, a wisdom and an energy such as that which a
Manichean would ascribe to his deity. Every where there are the marks
of deep design, but of design tending to evil and not to good. The
meanness of the end forms a singular contrast with the exquisite art
displayed in contriving the means. From the old government, and
from the revolution which had overthrown that government, every
thing was sedulously culled which could serve to make up a despotism
of the purest and most unmingled kind. The late shock had ascertained
the weak points of the ancient monarchy. On all those points the new
monarchy was fortified with peculiar care. It seemed that the most
tremendous convulsion ever produced by the spirit of liberty was to
serve no purpose except that of furnishing an artful tyrant with hints
which might enable him to construct an impregnable system of arbitrary power.

The republican spirit was not yet so completely extinguished in
France, that a young general could safely declare himself absolute at
once and without disguise. It was necessary that, for a time at least, the
rising despotism should be veiled by the semblance of a constitution.
Sieyès had acquired a high reputation for political science among the
revolutionists; and it was under cover of a plan of government proposed by Sieyès that the imperial tyranny was established.

That most profound and ingenious historian, M. Mignet, has given
a sketch of the constitution of Sieyès, illustrated by an intricate diagram.
The opinion of M. Mignet is entitled to great respect; but it is certainly
difficult to discover, either from his narrative, or from the labyrinth of
curves and triangles which he has called in to supply the deficiency of
language, what this constitution really was; and it is still more difficult
to discover any ground for the warm admiration with which he speaks

of it. A first magistrate who was to have the whole patronage of the state, and no power; ministers who were to have the whole power, and no patronage; a representative body chosen by a body of elected electors, out of a body of elected candidates; legislators appointed for short terms, who were to vote without speaking; tribunes appointed for life, who were to speak without voting; a conservative senate, of which one function was to have been that of ostracising eminent men; – such were some parts of the involved and cumbrous machinery devised by the oracle of French republicans. The sole principle of the constitution of Sieyès, as far as it is intelligible, seems to have been jealousy; jealousy of every thing and of every body, – of talents, – of popularity, – of the wealth of the few, – of the physical powers of the many. The first magistrate was to be a splendid state prisoner. Means were provided for reducing to insignificance every man whose abilities might seem likely to raise him to power. The mode in which the people were to elect their representatives was so circuitous, that there would, in fact, have been no representation at all. If this constitution had been really established and maintained, France would have been necessarily and constantly governed by mediocrity. The moment in which any man emerged to greatness would have condemned him to obscurity. The constitution of Venice bore a great resemblance to that which Sieyès proposed; and we know that Venice never produced a single great legislator, statesman, or general, – that she never produced even a single writer of the highest order. France under the constitution of Sieyès would have been among democracies what Venice was among aristocracies.

Undoubtedly, legislators ought to be jealous for liberty. But hypochondriac anxiety and precaution produce the same effects in the political as in the natural body. The health of governments, like the health of men, is rather benefited than injured by moderate exposure, and by change within certain limits. A state which, in order to preserve its institutions from all risk, prohibits the competition of talents and the shock of parties, like the valetudinarian who always keeps his hand on his pulse, who dines in a balance, and lives in an atmosphere regulated by the thermometer, escapes from some slight chances of danger at the price of certain languor and decay.

The constitution of Sieyès, however, though it might, like that of the year 1796,[1]* have been the constitution of France in name, could never have been so in reality. In times when law, as law, inspired scarcely any respect, it is clear that little restraint would be imposed on ambition and party spirit by a form of polity which could not be understood without a diagram.

It was a great object to Bonaparte to have on his side a name which all smatterers in politics were in the habit of pronouncing with mysterious reverence. He took the grotesque scheme of Sieyès as the basis of his new form of government. Those provisions which suited his ambitious designs were adopted; the rest was altered or rejected. The intricacy which characterised the original plan was preserved; and thus a constitution, which gave to the soldier of fortune power as absolute as that of Louis the Fourteenth, was promulgated as the work of a speculator who had carried his zeal for democracy to the length of regicide.

The only institution which, under the new system, had in any degree a popular character, was the tribunate; and this Napoleon abolished, when his power had been placed in perfect security by the victory of Austerlitz. The legislative body was the shadow of a shadow. The people chose by ballot electors for life; the electors chose candidates; and from among these candidates the senate chose the members of the legislature. The ballot boxes were confided to the local prefects. These officers were nominated by the emperor, and removable at his pleasure. They reported the result of the scrutiny exactly as they thought fit; and there is every reason to believe that they often reported it falsely. The senate, which chose the members of the legislature from among the candidates, was also under the absolute control of the emperor. The legislative body thus elected was prohibited from debating. Its only office was to give a simple affirmative or a simple negative to the propositions of the government; its conduct was such as might have been expected from the process by which its members were appointed, and from the rules by which its deliberations were restrained. The old parliaments of France, in spite of all the manifold defects of their

---

* All footnotes are editorial; there are none in Macaulay's text; see page 105.

constitution, often endeavoured, and not wholly without success, to impose some restraint on the kingly power. The legislative body under Napoleon was long the ready tool of arbitrary power and began to struggle for the liberty of France only when it had become difficult to struggle for her liberty without endangering her independence.

The old system of internal administration had passed away. The revolution had overthrown the local states, the parliaments, and the corporations; and all the powers, which under the fallen monarchy had been exercised by those authorities, passed entire to the central government. Thus the executive power, instead of being checked – as it is checked in many of those monarchies which we call absolute, – by bodies strong in ancient prescription and in the habitual veneration of the people, had at its command a vast army of public functionaries selected by itself, paid by itself, removable at its pleasure, and expecting promotion only from its favour. Spies and agents ready for every service were posted in every corner, and the fear of the omnipresent master of the state was on every inhabitant of the most secluded village.

The old ecclesiastical establishment had been utterly destroyed: to reconstruct it on its old foundations, would not have been for the interests of Napoleon; nor was it, indeed, in his power. Yet he was desirous to enlist on the side of his government those religious feelings which are so natural to the human mind, and which, having been almost extinguished in France under a corrupt and splendid hierarchy, had in some measure revived during the reign of blasphemy and terror. He accordingly established a church dependent on himself, and pensioned from the revenues of the state. Not only the clergy of the established religion, but all the ministers of all the Christian sects of his empire, were his stipendiaries. There was no teacher of religion in France, Catholic or Protestant, who did not know that his daily bread depended on the pleasure of the emperor. It is true, that the quarrel with the pope prevented Bonaparte from reaping all the advantage which he had expected from one of the most artful schemes ever devised for the support of power. This was not the only occasion on which the ingenuity of his plans were rendered unavailing by the childish violence of his passions.

The privileges of the old aristocracy had been utterly annihilated, and the memory of those privileges was held in abhorrence by all France. Bonaparte respected the work of the constituent assembly. He conferred, indeed, many favours on the old royalists, whom he considered as the natural allies of arbitrary power and the best teachers of courtly etiquette. But he never forgot, that though he was the founder of a monarchy, he was the creature of a revolution. He revived no ancient honours; but he created a new peerage and a new chivalry, bearing the same analogy to the old nobility which his pensioned and dependent church bore to the old ecclesiastical establishment. The old nobility had an existence and an importance of its own. It was coeval with the monarchy. Its immunities were protected by laws as venerable and prejudices as deeply seated as those which guarded the majesty of the throne, and were respected by the proudest and most absolute of the Bourbons. The new aristocracy was avowedly an aristocracy of upstarts. It had no dignity except what it derived from the preference of the sovereign. The very titles of the imperial dukes and princes present a remarkable contrast to those of the ancient nobles. The old appellations, taken from French domains, indicated that those who bore them were the proprietors and feudal lords of the soil of France. The new additions of honour came from the chronicles of the imperial victories. They were drawn from conquered provinces on the shores of the Adriatic, or from fields of battle in the heart of Italy, Germany, or Russia. It was impossible to hear them or to utter them without being reminded of the genius and power of him of whose glory all the honours of the state were but a faint reflection.

But the most formidable of the instruments which were at the command of Napoleon was that immense and magnificent army, at the head of which he appeared in fifty fields of pitched battle. Never was there competition so free, or prizes so high, or zeal so ardent, as in the military profession under this great leader. Glory and promotion were open to all; and one man was the supreme dispenser of glory and promotion. By promotion was meant not merely a company, or a regiment, or even the staff of a marshal. Rewards surpassing those which were won by the heroes of old romances, the hands of princesses, the thrones of great kingdoms, every thing that the world can offer, seemed to be within the reach of the young conscript, if once his services should attract the notice of his master. One French soldier reigned at Naples, another at Stockholm. The crown of Portugal, it was believed, was destined to be the reward of a third. It is not strange that the flower of a brave and ardent people should press emulously forward to take the most desperate risks of a lottery which held out the hope of prizes like these. The armies of France followed their chief with a confidence, a zeal, and a constancy, to which even the history of religious delusions scarcely furnishes a parallel. His word of exhortation or reprimand did more than the paradise of Mahomet or of Oder could do. Privation, defeat, captivity, wounds, the last agony, could not overcome this generous fanaticism. In the most dreadful nights of the retreat from Moscow, the frozen and starving fugitives repressed their murmurs when the emperor came within hearing. On the most bloody fields of battle, the dying waved their caps and shouted, if the emperor passed by. When, at the close of the war, the French prisoners were set at liberty in England, it was in vain that the people of the towns through which they were conveyed tried to bribe them to cry, 'Long live the Bourbons!' They obstinately answered, 'Long live the emperor!' None but a great man could have inspired so strong an attachment; none but an unfeeling and selfish man would have so cruelly abused it.

Such was the constitution of this mighty empire. The whole power, legislative, executive, judicial, and ecclesiastical, was virtually united in a single hand. The clergy of every persuasion, the civil functionaries of every kind and of every degree, all the officers and soldiers of the largest and finest army in the world, were absolutely at the command of one man. Young as his power was, it was more ancient than any of the other institutions of the state, and was the source, and the only source, of them all. He had nothing to fear from any internal movement in favour of the Bourbons. The old monarchy had passed away as completely as those pre-adamite worlds of which the inhabitants are known to us only by their fossil remains. Between the ancient system and that which had succeeded to it, had intervened an utter dissolution, a chaos, a new creation.

Yet the power of Napoleon, though greater than that of the most absolute sovereigns of Christendom, was exposed to one fearful danger, – a danger to which the Bourbons had paid but little regard, but which could not escape the notice of the heir of the revolution. The new government had risen on the ruins of an ancient and celebrated monarchy, which had fallen before the progress of the human intellect. The spirit which had produced the revolution, which had changed the whole constitution of society in France, and had given battle to all the monarchies of Europe, was not wholly extinct; and, as the calamities of anarchy faded from the remembrance of the people, would probably become stronger and stronger. To destroy it utterly, to prevent it from ever reviving, to turn the minds of men into a course different from that in which they had moved during the greater part of the eighteenth century, was the chief object of the policy of Napoleon. He is said to have observed that nobody could conceive the difficulties of governing a people who read the social contract and the spirit of laws.[2] His whole conduct showed that he was possessed by an ambition at once the meanest and the most gigantic that ever entered into any heart. Too selfish to govern in conformity with the liberal principles of the age, he attempted to compress the spirit of the age into conformity with his maxims of government. Political science was to be forced backwards. The public mind of Europe was to sink into second childhood, lest the depraved ambition of one man should encounter a single obstacle.

A system of education suitable to the system of government was established. The press was placed under the most severe and watchful restraint. The jealousy of the emperor was not confined to the writings of the living, but extended to works which had long been classical. Louis the Fourteenth, though a despot and a conqueror, had listened with respect to the noble discourse in which the eloquence of Massillon exposed the folly and wickedness of ambition. Bonaparte dreaded the effect which those sermons might produce on a people exhausted by taxes and conscriptions. Louis the Fourteenth, superstitious as he was, defended the Tartuffe of Molière against the hypocrites and bigots of his court. Bonaparte expressed his regret that such a piece should be in possession of the stage, and declared that, if it had been new, he would not have suffered it to be performed. Coming after a revolution produced by the force of public opinion, he was more competent than any of his predecessors to estimate that force, and was more solicitous than any of them to guard against it. He favoured architecture, sculpture, and the certain sciences. No exertions which the human mind could make in those quarters could endanger his power. But he detested metaphysics and political economy. He kept poetry under strict restraint. Every writer of every age who had set forth the evils of despotism he regarded as his personal enemy. He spoke with bitterness of the masterly portraits of Tacitus, of those lessons of benevolence which are conveyed in the sweet and glowing language of Fénélon, and of those bold attacks on political and social abuses which form the redeeming part of the writings of Voltaire. He hated madame de Stael, and persecuted her with unmanly cruelty. Other despots were content to prescribe to their subjects what they should not write; the French emperor dictated almost the whole literature of France: he made it a crime not to flatter him. All the food of the public mind was poisoned with adulation and falsehood; the little histories and catechisms of children were systematically tainted with servile doctrines. The people were suffered to know only so much of passing events as it might please their master to tell them, or as might come to their knowledge by vague report. The ablest and most powerful of European sovereigns degraded himself to the level of a common spreader of false news, and did not scruple to perform even with his own tongue and pen drudgery as infamous as that to which hunger drives the scribblers of disreputable journals. The bulletins of the army, and the reports of the imperial minister of war became proverbial for shameless disregard of truth. Such were the low arts to which a great man was compelled to stoop, to the gratification of a low ambition. Despotism was his object; and he saw that, in an age in which opinion is all-powerful, despotism must have its foundation in falsehood. The severity with which he persecuted writers whom he feared was not limited by the boundaries of the French empire. The liberty of thought could lurk in no corner of Europe to which he did not pursue it with inexorable hatred. By a cruel act of vengeance, he gave warning to the free spirit of German speculation. But the object of his most harassing fear and of his most deadly hatred was that great country from which France and Europe had learned to reason, – the mother of Locke, the nurse of Montesquieu and Voltaire. The literature, the history, and the laws of England had given the first impulse to that spirit which had overthrown the house of Bourbon. They might again

57

awaken that spirit; they might produce another revolution, and lay in the dust a yet more powerful and splendid monarchy. Had England been as far from France as the United States of America, or had the French been as ignorant and as bigoted as the Russians and the Austrians, the emperor might have disregarded the publications of English writers; but it was not easy to keep an intelligent people in ignorance on subjects which were freely discussed within a few miles of their own coast, by those whom they had already been accustomed to regard as their political instructors.

The war between England and Bonaparte, was on both sides, as least as much a war of passion as of policy. It was the conflict of two hostile principles. In the constitution of France and that of England there was absolutely nothing in common. The French government was a despotism sprung from a revolution: the English government was a limited monarchy, consecrated by immemorial prescription. In France there was more of social equality than in England; but in England there was political liberty, which was utterly wanting in France. Some great advantages France undoubtedly possessed over England; – the perfect toleration of all religious sects, – an uniform civil administration, – and the code. The revolution had swept away the whole of the ancient jurisprudence: the task of legislating anew necessarily devolved on the first stable government which arose in France; and Napoleon performed that task with great ability and success. The British islands were distracted by religious factions. Persecuting laws, now happily repealed, pressed down the fourth part of the population. The internal administration abounded with irregularities produced by the feudal or corporate privileges. Much of the law was unwritten; what was written was undigested. In these respects France had a decided advantage. But that advantage was far more than compensated by other circumstances. In England, the nation was something: in France, the government was every thing. In England, there was a legislative assembly, the composition of which was not indeed unobjectionable, but in which there was perfect freedom of debate, and in which there were always many members chosen by the people, and many others eager to acquire the approbation of the people. There was a free press. There was freedom of speech. There was personal freedom. In France, there was a silent representative body, a fettered press, and an army of spies. New state prisons had succeeded to the Bastile; and the mandate of the executive government was sufficient warrant for arrest and for detention.

The hatred with which the English people regarded Bonaparte can be conceived only by those who have felt it. The aristocrats hated him as an upstart; the democrats hated him as a tyrant. The great body of the nation, in whose minds, as in their institutions, two hostile principles are blended, – who love liberty, but whose love of liberty has a strong tinge of aristocratical feeling, – detested alike the despotism which he had established, and the anarchy from which he had sprung. As they had been almost constantly at war with France since the death of Louis the Sixteenth, they were ignorant of its internal state; they knew nothing of the real advantages which the great body of the population had derived from the abolition of privileges. The revolution was closely associated in their minds with the crimes and horrors of the reign of terror. They hated Bonaparte with a two-fold hatred, as the representative of two opposite evils. They had forgiven Washington; for America, like England, was free. They had honoured and lamented Louis XVI; for his power was, like that of the king of England, founded on an old constitution. But the jacobin emperor, the revolutionist who had destroyed liberty, the absolute sovereign who could show no ancient title, was to them an object of unmingled disgust.

Bonaparte fully returned their abhorrence. During the short space which followed the treaty of Amiens, the attacks of English writers had wounded his pride and excited his apprehensions. When the war recommenced, the vast power of England, though often ill directed, annoyed him every where. The pertinacity of her opposition goaded him almost to madness. He filled his state papers with abusive language, from which he would have refrained, if the violence of his passions had left him any sense of what was due to his dignity and to his political interests. All the presses of the continent were at his command, and he directed them all against England. In this contest he was not fortunate. The press of England, though free, was as unanimous as it would have been if directed by the government, and was infinitely more effective.

The power of France and that of England were different in kind, and could scarcely be brought to bear directly upon each other. France could conquer nothing from England. England could not prevent France from making vast conquests on the continent. The French armies entered every capital from Moscow to Lisbon. The English fleets blockaded every port from Dantzic to Trieste. On land, Napoleon was all-powerful. Wherever there were a few miles of sea, there was the empire of England. Sardinia, Sicily, Guernsey, and Jersey, remained perfectly secure during a war in which the whole continent was over-run by the French soldiers. No direct attack could be made on England. But trade was the strength of England; and Bonaparte resolved to make war upon trade. Human nature rose up against this last excess of tyranny. The allies, the very brothers of the emperor, attempted in vain to move that inexorable will. He deposed the most amiable of his brothers. He made war on the most valuable of his allies.

If the plans of Napoleon had succeeded, if he had been able to humble Russia, to drive the English from Spain, to keep down the whole continent by military force, if his life had been prolonged to the full age of man, and if his power had lasted as long as his life, it is scarcely possible to estimate the amount of evil which he would have produced. He would have renewed, perhaps for centuries, the expiring lease of tyranny. He would have substituted for the feudal monarchy of the Bourbons a monarchy on the more simple pattern of the east. The equality which the revolution had established amongst Frenchmen would have been merely the equality of the Turks. The insolence of office would have succeeded to the insolence of birth. The old aristocracy would have fallen, only that a new aristocracy, of the basest and most pernicious kind, might rise in its stead; an aristocracy of placemen, oppressing the people, and oppressed by each other. A new generation would have grown up skilfully trained and broken in to slavery, – a generation which would have derived all its political notions from books mutilated by censors, and conversations watched by spies. The government would have been like that of the Byzantine empire, or that of China, – a vast official hierarchy, rising by numerous gradations, with an oppressed people beneath and a solitary tyrant at the summit; and the human intellect would have languished as it languished under the emperors of the east, and as it has for ages languished in China.

But the plans of Bonaparte did not and could not succeed. In 1812 he seemed to be at the highest point of power. But his ruin was even then almost inevitable; from within, if he concluded a general peace; from without, if he remained at war. He had weaned

[one page missing]

empire fell even more rapidly than it had arisen. An immense army perished in the snows of Russia. Germany rose on its oppressors with one of those convulsive efforts of patriotic enthusiasm which constitute the noblest and most precious part of the history of mankind. The lieutenants of Napoleon were driven from Spain, and were unable to defend even the frontiers of France. In the autumn of 1812 the French armies had occupied Moscow and Madrid. In the autumn of 1813 eight hundred thousand enemies were preparing to pour over the Pyrenees and the Rhine.

In the midst of the general dismay the legislative body attempted to effect a reform in the state. That body had hitherto been – what its constitution necessarily made it – a tool in the hands of the emperor. A succession of disasters had taken away much of the terror which his name had inspired; and the representatives ventured to break that silence which the constitution of the empire imposed upon them.

Bonaparte demanded their sanction to those measures of national defence which the approach of the allied armies rendered necessary: under other circumstances his demand and their consent would have been mere matter of form. On the present occasion they intrusted the task of preparing an answer to a commission, the very selection of which indicated a spirit of opposition. Among the commissioners was a man whose name occupies a conspicuous place in the history of France since the restoration, – M. Lainé. That statesman has exerted himself with equal zeal on the side of the revolution, and on the side of the counter-revolution; yet malice itself has not ventured to impute any part of his conduct to unworthy motives. The most skilful delineators of his character have remarked, that his reason has always been under the tyranny of an irritable, though a generous, temper; and of a vivid, though not an original, imagination, – that whatever is grand or pathetic readily subjugates his mind, – that thus the enthusiasm of loyalty and the enthusiasm of liberty actuate him alternately; that each of these feelings during the period of its dominion almost wholly excludes the other, – and that, like most of those whose opinions are determined, not by argument but by taste and feeling, he is intolerant of contradiction, and considers it as a crime in others to defend against him that which he had himself defended but a short time before, and which he will soon defend again. Those who have thus represented him have allowed that he is emphatically an honest man; that he has atoned for his extraordinary inconsistency by a still more extraordinary disinterestedness; that even when placed in the most corrupting situations, and surrounded by the worst and basest allies, he has preserved an independent spirit, strict morals, simple manners, the most shining purity of personal honour, a noble contempt of offices, titles, and emoluments, and a true and fervent love of his country.

While the power of Napoleon was at its height, M. Lainé had exerted himself to raise an opposition in the legislative body: his efforts had failed. The recollection of two disastrous campaigns, and the dread of immediate invasion, now disposed the majority of his colleagues to second his plans. He took upon himself the dangerous office of reporting in the name of the commission. The language which he employed was such as had not been heard for years from any public man in France. It was necessary, he said, that the emperor should declare his intention of respecting the independence of foreign nations, and that liberty should be restored at home. The assembly resolved, by a great majority of ballot, that the report should be printed.

But the legislative body was not the states-general, nor had it to deal with Louis XVI. Though vanquished abroad, the emperor was still master in his own capital. The assembly was dissolved, and its hall closed without the slightest resistance. The spirit which broke forth in 1789, – and which revived with all its original energy, but with an energy moderated by wisdom and humanity, in 1830, – was utterly extinct.

The same sluggishness which the people had shown in defending their liberty, they showed also in defending their independence. The saying of Montesquieu was signally verified, – that despots resemble those savages who cut down the tree in order to eat the fruit. The northern armies deluged Champagne. The duke of Wellington conquered Gascony. The Austrians advanced on Lyons. The emperor appealed in vain to that national spirit which he had broken, and was astonished not to find the self-devotion of freemen in those whom it had been the aim of his whole policy to tame down into slaves. He put forth all the powers of his military genius. The remains of his army, outnumbered as they were, maintained their old reputation; but the nation, that impetuous and warlike nation, which, twenty years before, had triumphed over Europe, amidst misrule, bankruptcy, and famine, seemed to have disappeared from the face of the earth.

The hopes of the royalists began to revive amidst the dangers of the state. The zealous royalists indeed were few: but the power of a few zealous men in times of general languor and depression is immense. They were joined by persons whose influence and whose political skill far surpassed their own; persons who, though they felt no enthusiastic attachment to the house of Bourbon, saw in the restoration of that house the best means of securing peace with Europe on honourable terms, and of establishing in France a system of government which might unite the blessings of liberty with those of order. At the head of this class of persons stood a disgraced minister of Napoleon, – M. de Talleyrand, the most celebrated wit, courtier, and negotiator of his time. The public life of that celebrated man had not been free from the stains which, in times of frequent and violent change, are almost necessarily contracted by politicians. But it is just to say, that, if he was unfaithful to particular parties and particular families, he was in the main faithful to the interests of his country and to the great principles of government; that, though a revolutionist, he was never a jacobin; and that, though a minister of Napoleon, he had no share in the worst parts of the imperial tyranny.

The events of the war favoured the plans of the royalists. Bonaparte formed the bold project of taking the invaders in the rear, and cutting off their communications with Germany. He left Paris feebly defended. The allied armies advanced. The French troops whom they met retreated before them. Maria Louisa fled with her child to Blois. The court broke up. The capital was in confusion. The middle classes formed themselves into a national guard; but they were poorly armed and wholly undisciplined. The multitude clamoured for weapons; but the recollections of that terrible dominion which they had exercised twenty years before was still fresh, and their demand was rejected. A scanty force was assembled on the heights of Montmartre. It was composed of about 20,000 regular soldiers and of 4000 or 5000 citizens. The allied army consisted of nearly 200,000 excellent troops.

The event of this unequal conflict could not be doubtful. The French generals led back their troops from the heights, and concluded a capitulation, by which they agreed to evacuate Paris. It was on the evening of the 30th of March 1814 that the city was abandoned by its defenders. It had been arranged that the allies should take possession of it on the succeeding day.

The night was a time of anxious reflection. The retribution for years of merciless tyranny, for cities laid waste, for galleries of art plundered, for families dishonoured, was then, as it seemed, at hand. That a turn in the fortune of the war could take place appeared to be impossible. To obtain favourable terms of peace was all that the French people could expect; and it was probable that more favourable terms of peace would be granted to the old dynasty than to any other. The royalists took courage. Early in the morning of the 31st, white cockades and lilies were displayed in the streets, cries of 'Long live the king!' were heard, and papers severely reflecting on the imperial government were distributed. A meeting was held in the house of M. de Talleyrand. The task which that accomplished politician had undertaken, was indeed difficult. He had to unite in one party the men of the revolution and the men of the emigration, to prevail on regicides to concur in recalling the king, and on the three absolute monarchs who were at the gates of Paris to concur in a settlement which might secure the liberties of the people. His admirable skill surmounted or eluded every obstacle.

The allied sovereigns had, meanwhile, both in proclamations and in conferences, announced that the arms of Europe were directed, not against France but against Napoleon, and had invited the Parisians to assist in the work of establishing peace. The inhabitants of the capital, who had a few hours before expected to be given up to the rage of the Cossacks and the Prussians, were thus relieved from the most painful apprehensions. The humiliation which they were compelled to undergo seemed at the moment a blessing when compared with the fearful destruction which they had lately anticipated. The day of the entrance of the foreign armies was a day of rejoicing. The allied sovereigns were received with shouts by vast multitudes. Cries in favour of the Bourbons were raised by the zealous royalists, and echoed by many who, though they felt no attachment to the exiled family, considered the restoration of that family as a measure preliminary to an honourable and advantageous peace. The emperor of Russia took up his abode at the house of M. de Talleyrand, and appears to have been guided by the advice of his host.

That advice was most judicious. To restore the old dynasty without inflicting a cruel wound on the national pride was not easy. A government imposed by foreign sovereigns would be detested. Yet it was impossible at such a moment to consult the wishes of the people. The legislative body had been dismissed by Napoleon; but the senate still remained; and though that assembly neither deserved nor possessed the respect of the people, its intervention on the present occasion would at least spare to the French nation the most painful of all mortifications, and give to a change which was, in truth, produced by foreign invasion, something of the character of an internal revolution.

The allied sovereigns accordingly confined themselves to declaring that they would not treat with Bonaparte or with any member of his family, and left it to the senate to form a government with which they might be able to treat. That body immediately declared that Bonaparte had forfeited the allegiance of his subjects by his arbitrary measures. A provisional government was formed; many members of the legislative body assembled, and gave in their adhesion to the resolutions of the senate. A constitution was framed, and it was resolved that the crown should be offered to the exiled head of the house of Bourbon, on condition of his accepting this constitution, and swearing to observe it.

Napoleon, in spite of the revolt of his capital and his senate, was eager to try the chance of war again. His troops were ready to follow him. But several of his marshals, who had less to gain and more to lose than military men in lower stations, who were sick of war, and who shrank from the thought of civil conflict, refused to continue in his service. He offered to abdicate in favour of his son; and sent commissioners to open a negotiation on this basis with the allied sovereigns. Such was the dread which his name still inspired, that his offer, backed as it probably would have been by the Austrian government, might have been accepted, but for the sudden defection of Marmont. The emperor had raised that officer from obscurity, and patronised him in spite of some signal failures. Marmont now commanded the troops who had defended the heights of Montmartre against the allies. He had, after evacuating Paris, now retired to Essonne. As soon as he received intelligence of the transactions which had followed the entrance of the invaders into the capital, he treated for himself and his army with the provisional government, and with the foreign generals. A separate convention was speedily concluded; and the emperor was thus deprived of a force without the assistance of which it was absolutely impossible for him to renew the conflict. The negotiations between the commissioners of Napoleon and the sovereigns assembled at Paris were still pending when news arrived that the division commanded by Marmont had passed over to the allies. The offer of conditional abdication, which the commissioners had been charged to make, was now rejected; and the conquerors dictated their own terms. They required that Napoleon should resign for himself and his family the throne of France, and proposed to give him in return the island of Elba, with an ample revenue and the title of emperor.

After a short struggle, the fallen master of Europe stooped to accept these conditions. On the 20th of April he bade farewell to his guard, and left Fontainebleau for the place of his exile. The execrations of a people whom his conscriptions and his continental system had inflamed to madness pursued him through the southern provinces of France; those provinces through which he was soon to return in a strange and terrible triumph. In the mean time the senate had declared the count of Artois, lieutenant-general of the realm, till the arrival of his brother. On the 23d of April, Louis quitted London, amidst the acclamations of an innumerable multitude, and landed at Calais on the 24th, after a banishment of three and twenty years.

Between the restoration of Louis XVIII and the corresponding event in English history there are some marked points of contrast. Charles II was recalled by a parliament which spoke the sense of the whole people of England. He was received by his subjects with the most ardent affection. The form of government had undergone repeated changes; but the composition of society and the distribution of property had not been materially changed. The nation was the same nation that it had been in 1640, though in a different mood. It was, as it had been at the beginning of the civil dissensions, fond of monarchy and fond of liberty. But in 1640 it was suffering from the misconduct of the king, and in 1660 from the effects of a revolution. In 1640, therefore, the love of liberty predominated over loyalty; and in 1660, the sentiment of loyalty was more enthusiastic than the love of liberty. The nation had always been at heart friendly to royalty; but in 1640 it felt as a friend feels during a quarrel; and in 1660, as he feels at the moment of reconciliation. The death of Charles I was remembered with horror. The austerity of the puritans had made them unpopular. The restoration of the king was the restoration of healths, games, dances, and stage plays. There was nothing in the circumstances of that event which could wound the national pride. England concluded her first great revolution, as she had commenced it, without assistance or hinderance from abroad. She was dreaded and respected by all foreign powers: but she was torn by factions at home; and between those factions the heir of her ancient kings seemed to be the natural peace-maker.

Louis was invited to assume the crown of France as a peace-maker, not between hostile parties within, but between the nation and an overwhelming force from without. His restoration was not expressly required as a condition of peace: nor would the allies, in all probability, have insisted on it, if the public sentiment had been violently opposed to it. But it was clear that princes who had suffered so severely in their contests with the revolutionary governments of France could not look without great jealousy on the revival of the republic, or on the continuation of the empire. They certainly would not see, without great uneasiness, the elevation of any of those generals whose titles were drawn from fields of battle disastrous to Europe; whose military talents were inferior only to those of Napoleon; and who, if placed on the throne, would probably be desirous, after a short interval of repose, to efface the memory of recent defeats by the glory of another Austerlitz or Jena. In the situation, and in the disposition of the Bourbons, the conquerors could place full confidence. To the Bourbons they might safely grant terms, which the event of the war scarcely authorised the French to expect. The nation would remain in the first rank of European powers, and would retain, with the whole of its old territory, all the trophies of its recent victories. The restoration of the Bourbons was thus a most desirable event for France, as far as the foreign relations of France were concerned. It was the means, perhaps the only means, of preventing the military occupation or dismemberment of her territory, and the spoliation of the Louvre. It was the only expedient by which bitter humiliations could be averted. Yet that such an expedient should be necessary was in itself an humiliation.

The state of public feeling in France with respect to the restoration of Louis differed widely from the state of public feeling in England at the time of the restoration of Charles II. Louis returned to a people who knew not him nor his house. The France on which he had again set his foot was not that France which he had formerly known. The violent and searching revolution, which had driven him into exile, had, during his absence, done the work of ages. The ecclesiastical constitution, the civil administration, the geographical boundaries, had been changed. The limits of the old provinces had been effaced. The privileges of the old aristocracy had passed away. A new body of proprietors held the soil by a new tenure. A new jurisprudence was administered by a new magistracy. A new people – new in their opinions, their prejudices, and their social relations, – had sprung into existence. Between the living generation and that which had preceded it there was a great gulf, such as that which separates the modern nations of Europe from those great civilised societies which flourished before the northern invasion.

The government of Bonaparte, though not a free government, was a revolutionary government. He had derived his title from the revolution: his power, indeed, if it had lasted much longer, would probably have generated new evils, not less terrible than those from which the constituent assembly had delivered the people. But it had lasted just long enough to consolidate the work of the revolution; to fortify the new social system by an alliance with law, order, and religion. The Jacobins had merely demolished the old institutions: Bonaparte had erected new institutions on the ruins, and had thus rendered it impossible to restore the ancient fabric without a second demolition. In his person the revolution had assumed the character of legitimacy; had been acknowledged by all the governments of the civilised world; had been anointed by the successor of St Peter, and wedded to the daughter of the Cæsars.

Thus the royal emigrants returned to a country in which they could recognise nothing; to a country which still presents, in every part, to the eye even of a passing stranger, the signs of a great dissolution and renovation of society. They returned to find all that had been great and splendid in their youth passed away; to find sumptuous town houses broken up into lodgings; venerable sepulchres collected in museums; dismantled castles, defaced monuments, neglected cathedrals; a fountain playing on the spot where Richelieu had placed the statue of his master; a blank space where Henry IV had overlooked the Seine; a cotton mill standing on the ruins of Marli; a mound of turf heaped over the embalmed kings of St Denys; desolation in the fairy gardens of Chantilly, and silence in the gorgeous halls of Versailles. The magnificent trophies of a new dynasty filled their galleries, adorned their public places, and constantly reminded them that they were strangers in the palaces of their fathers. The seven sleepers of the ecclesiastical legend could scarcely have opened their eyes on a world more completely new to them.

The most distinguished of those who had recalled the old family, never intended to recall with that family the old order of things. The senators, in fact, did not recognise Louis, but elected him, and elected him on conditions. They decreed that he should be king if he would swear to the constitution which they had drawn up. The title which they offered to him was not that of king of France, but that of king of the French, which the constituent assembly had bestowed on his brother. They wished, to use a phrase of English law, that he should take the crown as a purchaser, and not by descent – as the heir of the revolution, not of Hugh Capet.

The proceedings of the senate disappointed and alarmed the remains of the old aristocracy. That aristocracy had been borne down and prostrated by the violence of the revolution. When tranquility was

restored, many emigrants returned to their country, and were suffered
to take possession of those parts of their estates which had not yet
been sold. Some of these men paid assiduous court to the emperor,
and comforted themselves for the downfall of the house to which they
had professed the warmest attachment, by reflecting that they still
had a despotic master to flatter. But though the old nobles were ready,
for the most part, to transfer their homage to the new dynasty, they
looked with unmixed aversion on the new social system. The revolution
had been a struggle, not so much between the nation and the king,
as between one caste and another: it was the rising up of millions of
the oppressed against thousands of oppressors. The primary object of
that great movement was the destruction of aristocratical privileges;
the destruction of the monarchy was merely a collateral incident.

Under Napoleon, the counter-revolutionary party was weak and
almost imperceptible; it seemed to acquiesce peaceably in the great
change which had passed on society: but the restoration quickened the
sluggish faction into life and malignant energy. The enemies of the
revolution began to hope that the aristocracy might rise, as it had
fallen, with the throne. The restoration of the old dynasty would not
satisfy them without the restoration of the old system: they pined for
the France of their youth, – the provinces, the bailliages, the local
states, the parliaments, the feudal tenures, the tithes, the abbeys, the
old honours of nobility, the old orders of knighthood. They even seemed
to regret the dungeons and seraglios of their old tyrants. They often
expressed their aversion to the guillotine, and their wish that the wheel
and the gallows might be restored. In order that the king might be
able to restore their privileges, they were eager to restore all his
prerogatives. According to them, the revolution, and all the governments which had sprung from the revolution, were unlawful: the
rightful sovereignty had always resided in the person of the head of
the house of Bourbon, – in that of Louis XVI at the bar of the convention; in that of Louis XVII under the scourge of a brutal master;
in that of Louis XVIII at Mittau, or at Hartwell.[3] No election was
needed: no condition could be imposed. The act of the senate added
nothing to the rights of the lawful prince: if it were his good pleasure
to give a constitution to his subjects, such a proof of his royal benignity

ought to be thankfully received; but that the senate, a body instituted by a man who had himself no title but that of force, should compel the king to purchase by concessions a crown which was already his own by inheritance, was the most atrocious of treasons.

Such was the language which the violent partisans of the Bourbons addressed to the allied sovereigns: the emperor of Russia, in particular, was besieged by them; but above all things they laboured to instil their doctrines into the mind of the restored king.

It cannot be denied that the principle of legitimacy, justly limited, is a natural and salutary principle. It is good for the people that there should be government. It may be doubted whether men are not less miserable under the worst government that exists, than they would be if there were absolutely no government at all. The time of transition, even from a bad to a good government, is generally a time of greater misery than the time which precedes it. England was surely in a worse state during the civil war than while the star chamber sate, and while the ship-money was exacted. France was in a worse state during the five years which followed the meeting of the states-general, than under madame du Pompadour, or madame du Barri. Even when a salutary change has been effected, some time must elapse before the new system acquires that authority and stability which the old system had possessed.

Revolution is, therefore, in itself an evil; – an evil, indeed, which ought sometimes to be incurred for the purpose of averting or removing greater evils, but always an evil. The burden of the proof lies heavy on those who oppose existing governments; nor is it enough for them to show that the government which they purpose to establish is better than that which they purpose to destroy. The difference between two systems must be great, indeed, if it justifies men in substituting the empire of force for that of law; in resolving society back into its original elements; in breaking all those associations which are the safeguards of property and order. Thus far the principle of legitimacy may be fairly carried; those who carry it further, those who represent it as an absolute and unbending principle, attack, not merely the liberty of nations, but the authority of all governments. There probably is not, in the whole world, a government in the title of which, if investigated according to the strict rules of legitimacy, flaws would not be discovered. If Bonaparte was an usurper so was Hugh Capet, and so was Pepin; yet there is, probably, no votary of legitimacy who would think it right to depose the Bourbons in favour of a pretender who might be able to make out, by the clearest evidence, his descent from the long-haired kings of the Merovingian race. If power, which originates in proceedings inconsistent with the laws, can never become lawful, Louis XVI had no more right to the French throne than Marat or Santerre. If power, unlawful in its origin, may by lapse of time become lawful, what length of time is necessary?

Those who hold highest the right of lawful governments to the obedience of nations cannot surely consider it as more sacred than the right of a man to his estate. But even with regard to property, all good codes have established a time of limitation, a time after which a title, however illegally acquired, cannot be legally set aside; and these provisions, far from making property insecure, do, in fact, add to its security. A system of laws, under which a man should be liable to be turned out of lands which had descended to him through a long line of ancestors, on account of some injustice committed during the wars of York and Lancaster, would be practically a system of licensed robbery. A landed proprietor would feel as a merchant feels among the Bedouins. He would never be sure that the day, which was passing over him, might not bring forth his ruin; and thus the law would, by its strictness, defeat the very end for which laws exist, and produce uncertainty and apprehension instead of security.

As in municipal law, too close a scrutiny into the original title by which property is held is inconsistent with those ends for which the institution of property exists, so in that higher law which regulates the relations of governments and societies, too close an adherence to the principle of legitimacy is destructive of all authority. Even those who are so unreasonable and narrow-minded as to deny that resistance to lawful governments can in any case be justifiable, must, as friends of order, admit that to the rights of governments, as to the rights of individuals, there must be a time of limitation. If this be not conceded, no power can be considered as lawful, and no rebel can ever want a pretext. The municipal law fixes its time of limitation with accuracy;

but at what time a government, unlawful in its origin, may fairly plead prescription, at what time the burden of the proof which originally lay on those who introduced the new system passes to those who wish to restore the old system, it is impossible accurately to determine. The period will vary according to the violence of the revolution and the movement of the public mind.

If we apply these principles to the case of France in 1814, we shall see great cause to regard the ultra royalists as enemies, not merely of liberty, which they never professed to love, but of law and order, which they have always represented as the greatest of blessings. The changes produced by the revolution were, for the most part, decidedly beneficial. The price paid for them had indeed been tremendous; but it had been paid; and there could be no reason for throwing the purchase away. If, in 1789, a wise and good man could have foreseen all the calamities through which the existing generation was about to pass, he would have thought it better to accept those concessions which the king and the aristocracy were disposed to offer, and to trust the rest to time and the progress of the human mind, than to make society pass through the agonies and convulsions of an utter dissolution, for the purpose of effecting a complete purification in a few years. But in 1814 this was not the question. The dissolution had taken place. The purification had been accomplished. Twenty-five years, into which the events of ages had been compressed, had covered with their mourning and with their trophies all that had of old been great in France. Men had lived years in every month. They no more resembled their fathers, than their fathers resembled the burghers of the League, or the peasants of the Jacquerie. Legitimacy, in the rational sense of the word, had crossed over to the side of the revolution. The old privileges could not be revived; the forfeited estates could not be restored; the ancient system of administration could not be re-established; the church could not again become rich and powerful, without another struggle, at least, as terrible as that from the effects of which society was still smarting. The ultra-royalists persisted in talking of revolutionary theories, as if they had been discussing the question of tithes, or of the veto in the constituent assembly. They would not see that the revolution was now not a theory, but a fact; that it was not an innovation, but an establishment; and that those who attacked it were the real revolutionists.

The king was placed in a very distressing situation. His nearest relatives were infected by the extravagant doctrines which we have been considering. Those persons who were loudest in protestations of attachment to his person urged him to assert the rights of a lawful king. To suffer his prerogatives to be wrested from him might seem pusillanimous; to abandon the interests of those who had suffered in his cause might seem ungrateful. His task was difficult; yet, in the history of his own family, he might have found an example well deserving to be studied and imitated. The first king of the branch of Bourbon ascended the throne under circumstances still more discouraging than those in which his descendant was placed. Henry IV was at the head of a party; and that party was a minority of the nation. He had faithful services to requite; he had deadly wrongs to avenge. The blood of his kinsmen and friends had been shed on the field of battle, or by the daggers of assassins. A massacre, which equalled in cruelty, and far exceeded in perfidy, the crimes of the revolution, had left a deep and bitter remembrance in his heart.[4] His capital was in arms against him. Civil war was raging throughout his dominions. Whether his claims would ever be established seemed very doubtful. That he should ever reign in peace, security, and popularity, seemed utterly impossible; yet, in a few years, that remarkable man conciliated his enemies without alienating his friends, and, in a great measure, effaced from the public mind the traces of the most horrible injuries ever inflicted or suffered by contending factions. He died the king of his whole people. He was followed to his grave with tears and lamentations, by the inhabitants of the very city which had most fiercely opposed him; and left a name which, even at this day, has not wholly lost its influence over the hearts of his countrymen.

Henry had effected these things by yielding to the force of circumstances, and putting himself at the head of the enemies of his house and party. He was thus enabled to serve the sect which he abandoned far more effectually than he could have served it if he had still been one of its members. The sacrifice which Henry made was indeed one which no man, justly impressed with the importance of religious truth, would have made for any temporal object. In this respect Louis XVIII was far more happily situated: he would have violated no religious duty, if he had acted towards the hostile factions of France on the principle on which Henry acted towards hostile sects.

Louis was by no means ill qualified to perform the part of his great ancestor. His understanding was excellent, his reading extensive, his temper mild and equal. He had no fanaticism political or religious. During the reign of his brother he had been one of those who wished to see the royal power restrained by constitutional checks. At the beginning of the revolution his conduct had given great offence to the violent royalists. To the last they continued to suspect him, and to consider his brother, the count of Artois, as their leader. The excesses of the French revolution had alienated from the cause of liberty many who had once been warmly attached to it. But no such effect had been produced on the clear judgment and serene disposition of Louis. Such as he had been in the assembly of the notables, he still, after all that he and his family had suffered, continued to be. He had some of those infirmities and faults which expose a sovereign to the derision of his contemporaries. His person was extremely ungraceful. Corpulence and disease almost prevented him from moving. He was frivolous in some of his tastes; and was extravagantly fond of the pleasures of the table. But history owes him this honourable testimony, that he struggled long against the influence of bad advisers; that he yielded to it only when sickness, age, and domestic calamities had broken the force of his mind; that the best measures of his reign were those which he was himself concerned in preparing, and that his best ministers were those of his own free choice.

He was, at his accession, under the necessity of making his election between the old and the new system, – of recognising or disallowing the revolution. Had the count of Artois been placed in the same situation, that prince would probably have perished in a frantic attempt to undo all that the constituent assembly had done. The duke of Orleans, on the other hand, would have sworn fidelity to the constitution prepared by the senate, and would have entered Paris with the tricoloured cockade in his hat, and the badge of the legion of honour on his breast. Louis took neither of these courses. A week after his arrival in France he issued, at St Omer,[5] a proclamation, announcing the principles on which he intended to act. In this document he promised to his subjects a free constitution, but refused to ratify that which had been offered to him.

'We have,' said he,[6] 'taken into our most serious consideration the plan of government proposed by the senate. Fully approving of the principle on which that plan has been framed, we have nevertheless felt that many of the articles bear evident marks of the haste in which they were drawn up, and ought not, in their present form, to become fundamental laws of our realm. It is our full purpose to establish a free constitution. It is our wish, in preparing that constitution, to proceed with prudence and deliberation. We cannot give our sanction to a plan which requires so much correction as that now proposed to us. We shall, therefore, undertake the office of preparing a constitution. We shall call to our assistance commissioners chosen from the senate and the legislative body; and we shall lay before those assemblies the fruits of our deliberations. The principles of the constitution shall be these: – There shall be a representative body. The legislature shall be divided into two houses; and no tax shall be imposed without its free consent. Public and private liberty, the liberty of the press, and the liberty of religious worship, shall be secured. Property shall be held inviolably sacred. The sales of national estates shall be declared irrevocable. The ministers shall be responsible. The judges shall be irremovable; the tribunals shall be independent; and every Frenchman shall be admissible to every office.'

The conduct of Louis, in taking the crown without fulfilling the conditions which the senate had imposed, excited some discontent, and would undoubtedly have excited much more, had the senators been respected by the nation. But they were men who had not been chosen by the people, and who, as a body, had done nothing to deserve the confidence of the people. They had been, with a few honourable exceptions, the most abject flatterers of Napoleon in the time of his greatness. They had insulted him at the moment of his fall. They had pronounced sentence of deposition on the author of their power; and had assigned, as reasons for that sentence, acts in which they had themselves been accomplices. They had inserted in the constitution presented by them to the king an article, the selfishness and impudence of which threw ridicule on the whole plan. They stipulated, that their own pensions should be held sacred; that they should continue to form the higher branch of the legislature; and that the senatorial dignity, which Napoleon had conferred on them only for their lives, should, with all the emoluments attached to it, be hereditary in their families. The public was moved to laughter and indignation, at seeing a provision which was designed solely for the profit and aggrandisement of a few hackneyed courtiers placed among the fundamental laws of the state; and many who wished that the constitution should be, not a royal grant, but a covenant between the king and the nation, were reconciled to their own disappointment by that of the senators.

On the third of May Louis entered Paris. The ceremony was gloomy, and full of evil omen. The king was unable, from the state of his health, to show himself to the people on horseback. His valetudinarian habits presented a striking contrast to the restless activity of Napoleon. The body of the population received him with sullen apathy, as a stranger whom they neither loved nor hated. The zealous friends of liberty were displeased with him for taking the crown as his birthright. The violent royalists, on the other hand, thought that the proclamation of St Omer promised far too much.

But there was another body in the procession far more important than the royalists or the republicans. Round the carriage of the king marched the old guard of Napoleon, that formidable band which never met its match till it crossed bayonets with the English grenadiers at Waterloo. Only a fortnight had elapsed since those impenetrable ranks had encircled the emperor. Betrayed by his marshals, deposed by his senate, abjured by his capital, abandoned by his family, he had found his guard faithful to the last. It was to them that he had addressed his parting words. It was to their eagle that he had given his parting embrace. At one sign from him they would, even in that moment of despair, have followed him against eight hundred thousand enemies. They were now encircling a prince whose elevation was inseparably associated in their minds with the disasters of the French arms, and whose talents and virtues were precisely those which inspire soldiers

77

with the least respect. They performed their military duty; but they performed it with sullen murmurs, and with looks of dark and resolute hatred. All eyes were turned on them, on the last defenders of France, on the last followers of the emperor. A cry of 'Long live the guard!' burst from the multitude, and almost drowned the cry of 'Long live the king!'

The first measure of the king was to form a ministry. At the head of it was placed M. de Talleyrand, whose services in the restoration of the Bourbons had been as conspicuous as those of Monk in the restoration of the Stuarts. Unfortunately, M. de Talleyrand, who was fitted beyond any man in France, by his talents and by his situation, to act the part of mediator between the old dynasty and the new people, was, soon after his elevation, under the necessity of repairing to the congress at Vienna. M. Louis, a gentleman of liberal opinions, and of great skill in matters of revenue, was appointed minister of finance. The other nominations were not equally judicious; and one of them was highly objectionable. General Dupont, whom Castanos had forced to capitulate at Baylen, and who had since that event been in disgrace, was made minister of war. There never were more contemptible enemies than those with whom general Dupont had been matched; there never was a discomfiture more complete than that which he had sustained; and it was, therefore, most unwise to place him at the head of a service to which belonged warriors who had shown themselves worthy rivals of Suwarrow, of the archduke Charles, and of Wellington. Peace was concluded on terms which, under all the circumstances, must be considered as highly advantageous to France. Her European territory was left somewhat larger than it had been before the revolution, and she was suffered to retain all the trophies of her conquests. Some of the French colonies were ceded to England; but it may be doubted, whether France has lost, or England gained, by the transfer.

The government was now at leisure to settle the question of the constitution. On the 4th of June, the legislative body and the senate were convoked, and the charter, in which were set forth the rights of the sovereign and of the nation, was solemnly read.

In the preamble of this memorable instrument it is laid down as a fundamental proposition, that all lawful power resides in the king alone.

The charter is represented as a concession granted by the spontaneous bounty of the royal mind. The year 1814 is reckoned as the 19th of the reign of Louis. Thus the revolution, and all the governments which had sprung from it, are branded with illegitimacy.

But though in the preamble and in the date of the charter the king might seem to lean towards the notions of the ultra-royalists, no such leaning appeared in the enactments. It was announced that all Frenchmen were equal before the law, were equally bound to contribute to the expenses of the state, and were equally admissible to all its honours; that full and impartial protection should be given to all religions; that the ministers of all Christian persuasions should still be maintained out of the public revenue; that no man should be deprived of his personal liberty, except in cases specified by law; and that every man should be at liberty to publish his opinions, provided that he confined himself within the limits which the law might assign to discussion. The sales of national property were recognised; the conscription was abolished; and a full and entire amnesty was granted for all offences committed before the restoration.

With the king remained the supreme executive power, and all the vast patronage which Napoleon had possessed. The royal person was declared sacred; but it was provided that the ministers should be responsible.

The legislative power was divided between the king and two assemblies, the chamber of peers and the chamber of deputies. The king alone could propose laws; but the chambers might request him to propose any law which they might think necessary. When a law had passed the chambers, it still required the definitive sanction of the king to give it validity.

The peerages might be either hereditary or for life: the right of conferring them belonged to the king alone. The deliberations of the chamber of peers were to be secret.

The most important part of the charter was that which regulated the constitution of the chamber of deputies; and it was also the most defective. The organisation of the electoral colleges was expressly reserved for future consideration. All that was at present enacted was, that no man should be an elector unless he had completed his thirtieth

year, and unless he paid 300 francs of direct taxes. It was not enacted
that all men of thirty who paid 300 francs of direct taxes should have
votes; so that on this subject, – a subject of vital importance in all
representative governments, – the charter contained only words of
exclusion.

It was provided, that no person should be a deputy until he had
completed his fortieth year. The sittings of the deputies were to be
public. The chamber was to be renewed by fifths annually; but the
king could at any time dissolve it.

The ministers might be members of either chamber: they were also,
as ministers, entitled to assist at the deliberations of both chambers, and
to be heard whenever they might think fit to speak.

The code of Napoleon was still to be the law of France, except in so
far as its provisions might be inconsistent with those of the charter.
The judges were to be irremovable. The judicial proceedings were to be
public. No extraordinary tribunal was to be established. The punishment of confiscation was never to be inflicted. The right of remitting
and commuting punishments was reserved to the king.

The titles of the old nobility were revived, and those bestowed by
Napoleon were confirmed: but no title was to exempt its possessors
from the ordinary obligations lying on citizens. The legion of honour
was to be kept up; the military pensions were to be continued; and the
national debt was declared sacred.

Lastly, it was provided that the legislative body which had sat under
Bonaparte should be the first chamber of deputies.

In this celebrated law the whole policy of Louis XVIII appears. That
policy seems to have been to lean towards one side in matters of form,
and towards the other in matters of substance; to gratify the royalists by
restoring the names and badges of the old government, and at the
same time to conciliate the body of the people by respecting, in all
important points, that order of things which the revolution had produced. Thus the king refused to accept the throne on conditions; but,
having taken possession of it as a right, he proceeded to grant as favours
what had been proposed as conditions. By styling himself Louis XVIII,
and by reckoning the year 1814 as the 19th of his reign, he declared that
he considered all the governments which had held power during his

exile as illegitimate; but he bound himself, at the same time, to discharge their debts and to execute their laws. He gave back to the old nobles the titles of which the constituent assembly had deprived them; but he held out to them not the faintest hope that their privileges of caste would ever be restored. In the same manner he assumed the title of Most Christian King, and called himself the eldest son of the church; but he had no intention of reinstating the priesthood in its ancient domains, or in its ancient power. The white flag and the lilies succeeded to the tri-colour and the eagle; but the old army remained embodied under the new colours. The revolution was not recognised; but the work of the revolution was preserved.

Upwards of 150 peers were created, many of whom had been marshals and senators of the empire. The legislative body, now the chamber of deputies, commenced its deliberations: M. Lainé was appointed president. A liberal civil list was voted, and large incomes were settled on all the members of the royal family.

The people felt but little respect for the assembly which was said to represent them. Under a new name, that assembly preserved its old character, and paid to the king the same servile obedience to which it had been trained under the despotic rule of the emperor. Accustomed to submission, it scarcely knew how to oppose. Accustomed to silence, it scarcely knew how to debate. Its tame acquiescence in the measures of the government soon produced fatal effects.

It was not to be expected that the charter would satisfy the partisans of the emperor, or the surviving jacobins; but if it had been faithfully observed, and followed up by a liberal and judicious law regulating the constitution of the electoral colleges, it would in all probability have satisfied the great body of the nation. Unhappily, about a month after the memorable day on which the charter had been promulgated, M. de Montesquiou, minister of the interior, and M. de Blacas, to whom belonged the direction of the royal household, and who was generally considered as the personal favourite of Louis, submitted to the deputies a law directly opposed to one of the most important articles of the charter: they proposed that newspaper, periodical works, and all books of fewer than thirty sheets, should be subjected to a censorship for the term of three years.

The eighth article of the charter was in these words : – 'It is the right of every Frenchman to publish and cause to be printed the opinions which he may hold, provided always that he conform himself to such laws as may be passed for the purpose of repressing the abuses of this liberty.'

To reconcile this article with a law establishing a censorship was no easy matter; and it would have been judicious in the government not to make the attempt, but to acknowledge the inconsistency, and to represent the necessity as urgent and the restraint as temporary. The best course would have been not to violate the charter; the next best course, to violate it openly. The ministers did their best to refine away the plain meaning of the article which they were desirous to suspend. A censorship was, according to them, a mode of repressing the abuses arising from the liberty of the press. The charter had announced that laws would be made for the purpose of repressing those abuses: this was such a law. If it were passed, the people would have all that had been promised them: they would be at perfect liberty to publish their opinions, provided always that they would conform to the regulation which directed them to obtain the approbation of a censor before they published their opinions. It is unnecessary to expose this base and shallow sophistry.

Louis, it is generally believed, had been earnestly entreated by his advisers to omit or modify the eighth article of the charter. But he had lived long in England. He knew that public peace and the authority of government are by no means incompatible with the utmost freedom of discussion; and he was resolute. It is true, that the situation of France differed widely from that of England. The authority of the government was new, and therefore precarious. The liberty of the press was new, and therefore produced violent excitement. The public mind, no longer compressed by the censorship, sprang up with a rapidity which appalled those who had taken away the restraint. The king ought to have been prepared for this. He ought to have known that, though the evils produced by the liberty of the press may, at first sight, appal and disgust one who is unaccustomed to them, yet for those evils the liberty of the press is itself the best and most certain cure. Above all, he should have considered that no discontent, which journals or satires could excite, would be so formidable as that discontent which he would himself excite by violating the charter within a month after he had given it. But his feelings had been wounded; his person and family had been attacked. His bad advisers renewed their solicitations, and assured him that the public mind would shortly be poisoned with calumny and sedition. He yielded; and his yielding on this occasion was the beginning of evils which mankind will long remember.

The opposition to the censorship was headed by M. Raynouard. That gentleman was known to Europe as the author of a tragedy worthy of the best age of the French drama. He had been one of that commission which, at the close of 1813, protested against the abuses of the imperial government. He now argued with distinguished ability and eloquence against the projected violation of the charter. The public mind was greatly excited. Vast crowds surrounded the hall in which the deputies met. The most fashionable and beautiful women of Paris mingled in the throng, and pushed their way through the sentinels: the crowd of strangers filled the galleries, and overflowed into the seats appropriated to the deputies. Such a spectacle had not for many years been seen in France.

The ministers agreed to introduce some modifications into the law, and with these modifications it passed both the chambers. Books of more than twenty sheets were exempted from its operation, and the term of its duration was shortened. But the great mischief had been done: the government had quibbled away one of the clearest and most important articles of the great national compact; and from that time forward all its measures were regarded by the people with a suspicion which, as respected Louis personally, was unjust, but which was by no means unnatural.

A panic arose among the purchasers of national domains. The revolutionary governments had been pronounced illegitimate. The title to a vast mass of property had been derived from those governments. The charter, while it declared the title bad, declared also that the possession should be undisturbed. But the charter had been violated, and might be violated again. The same subtlety, which had found a censorship in an article enacting the freedom of the press, might find restitution in the clause which confirmed the sales of national property. Royalist lawyers published pamphlets, in which the holders of the confiscated estates were designated as robbers. Several priests declaimed from the pulpit with great violence against those who had usurped the patrimony of the church. Sometimes the unfortunate proprietor was Achan, who had touched the accursed thing. Sometimes he was Ahab, who had unjustly seized the vineyard of the Jezreelite. One preacher pushed this last comparison very far, and assured the guilty members of his congregation, that dogs would infallibly lick their blood if they persisted in their iniquity. Many ecclesiastics refused to administer the sacraments to the holders of church lands. These things excited great alarm, and the conduct of the ministers was not calculated to dispel it.

The government proposed that those national estates which were still unsold should be restored to the ancient proprietors. In itself the proposition was unobjectionable, and, if sufficient guarantees had been given to the revolution, would probably not have been unpopular; but the charter was the only title-deed by which many thousands of square miles were held, and one of the most important covenants of the charter had been broken.

The language of the priests and of the old nobles had exasperated the nation. It was apprehended that the partial restoration now proposed might be merely the prelude to a general restoration. The ministers represented their measure as a measure not of grace, but of absolute justice. They protested against the use of the word emigrant. That word, they said, described falsely and injuriously a class of good and patriotic Frenchmen, whom tyranny had driven beyond the local boundary of France, but who had been unalterably attached to her interests. This language was most imprudent. It was clear that the French people could not acquit the emigrants without condemning themselves. The memory of the army of Condé was still held in abhorrence; and, though it was not to be expected that the Bourbons should in this respect sympathise with the national feeling, it was unwise in them to outrage it.

The panic spread from the proprietors to the labourers. The French peasantry were in a far happier condition than they had ever known before the revolution. They were better lodged, better clothed, and better fed. The improvement had, undoubtedly, been in a great measure produced by the abolition of those oppressive privileges which anciently depressed industry. It was now whispered that the old feudal rights were to be restored with the old feudal lords. A feeling of disaffection spread through the agricultural population. The people of the commercial towns, who had suffered less from the old monarchy, and more from the revolution and the war with England, than the inhabitants of the country, showed in general less anxiety.

Some of the regicides who had sat in the conservative senate, and who had concurred in the vote which recalled the Bourbons, were treated with marked indignity. On the other hand, honours and rewards were bestowed on the chiefs of the Vendean insurrection. It is impossible to blame Louis for looking with aversion on those who took away the life of his gentle and virtuous brother, or for feeling gratitude to the devoted adherents of his house; but at the same time it is impossible to blame his subjects for looking on his proceedings with great uneasiness. The sentence passed on Louis XVI was, indeed, most cruel and unjust. But many persons had concurred in it, of whose general character cruelty and injustice formed no part. Enthusiasm, prejudice, party spirit, the sense of imminent public danger, had swelled the majority with the names of many men whose subsequent conduct proved their sincerity, and redeemed their error. But even had it been otherwise, the king had promised oblivion, not pardon. The expressions of the charter were remarkably strong. 'We enjoin this oblivion,' said the king, 'on our tribunals, and recommend it to all our subjects in their individual capacity.' Was it for the sovereign, who had recommended perfect reconciliation, to set the first example of vindictive remembrance? Were the chronicles of the revolution to be opened? Were the votes and speeches of twenty-five disastrous years to be noted for punishment or reward? If some young and ardent enthusiast had exulted in the fall of the Bastile, had fancied that he saw in the triumph of the national assembly the dawn of a golden age of liberty and reason, had felt his spirit rise up against foreign interference, and had been willing to stand by the worst government that the jacobin club could set up, rather than expose France to the fate of Poland, was he now, when sobered by the experience of a long and eventful life, –

he loved his country as well as formerly, but more wisely, – to be called to account for votes given and expressions employed in a time of intense excitement, of passionate hopes and fears, of conspiracies, of seditions, of foreign and intestine war? The courage and fidelity of the Vendeans had, indeed, been admirable; but it was against the great body of their countrymen that they had been courageous; it was to a family, and not to the nation, that they had been faithful. To confer public honours on them was to declare that the reigning family was every thing, and the nation nothing. The king owed them a debt of gratitude; but it was a private debt, and should have been privately paid. The civil list, and the vast patronage of the crown, would have enabled him to gratify those who had distinguished themselves by their attachment to his house, without exciting the indignation of the people. Ostentatious honours paid to the champions of one party were insults to all the members of the other.

The count of Artois, while acting as lieutenant-general of the kingdom before the arrival of his brother, had promised that certain oppressive taxes, analogous to our excise, should be abolished. The promise was rash; and when the state of the finances, which under the government of Napoleon had been carefully concealed, came to be understood, it was clear that the performance was impossible. The people accused the Bourbons of a breach of faith. Their murmurs were natural; but it is only just to admit that the error was in making the engagement, and not in breaking it.

Louis was by no means a fanatic in religion; but he could not restrain the imprudent zeal of his followers. A whole generation had passed away since the government had interfered to compel the observance of religious duties. The police now insisted on the rigorous observance of the Sunday. It is clear that laws on such a subject, unless they are supported by a strong public feeling, much produce an effect directly the reverse of that which they are designed to produce.

This was not all. A respectable actress died at Paris; and Christian burial was refused to her. The absurdity and barbarity of this proceeding excited great indignation. Vast multitudes assembled: the doors of the church were forced; and serious consequences were

86

apprehended. The king very judiciously interfered, and prevailed on the priests to give way. But it was well known that the clergy exercised boundless influence over the presumptive heir to the throne, and over a large portion of the ultra-royalist party. Every fault, therefore, committed by the clergy injured the cause of the Bourbons.

But nothing inflamed the public discontent so much as the insolence with which some of the old nobility enjoyed their triumph over the body of the nation. Many of these men had accepted their pardon and their property from Napoleon. Some of them had solicited posts in his household, and had taught the pompous etiquette which they had studied at Versailles in their youth to the ragged soldiers of the imperial aristocracy. Some had just returned from a long exile with minds enslaved by all the prejudices of the old court, and hearts burning with all the passions of the first emigration. These men pronounced the word 'charter' with a sneer, and hinted that Louis was an atheist and a jacobin, and joined to the acclamations of their loyalty a significant phrase, which indicated that the king had no personal claims to their attachment. They always spoke of the count of Artois as the model of a French prince, and added no invidious qualification to the sincere wishes which they breathed for his life. Proud of ancient honours, which in the minds of the people were associated with ideas of feudal tyranny, they looked with contempt on those more modern titles, the sound of which awakened recollections of the victories of France, – recollections doubly precious in the day of her humiliation.

But the circumstances which, far more than any other, rendered the Bourbons unpopular, was the manner in which they had been recalled. The degradation of France had been their elevation. However artfully the policy of M. de Talleyrand and the generosity of the allies might disguise the fact, every man knew and felt that he lived under a sovereign imposed on him by foreigners. While vast armies of invaders were encamped on the banks of the Seine and the Garonne the French were disposed to purchase the evacuation of the territory at any price. But now the invaders had departed; the prisoners had returned. The danger was over; but the humiliation remained. The national pride rose up fiercer and stronger from its brief intermission. It seemed hard, almost intolerable, that the fruit of so many years of glory should be a dynasty imposed by strangers, and a boundary falling far within the Rhine.

Yet, though solemn pledges had been forfeited, though the charter had been violated almost as soon as it had been given, though the purchasers of the national estates were uneasy, though the peasantry murmured, though the bigotry of the priests and the arrogance of the old nobles excited strong resentment, though the circumstances under which the restoration had been effected were galling to the feelings of every patriotic Frenchman, still the great body of the people shrunk from the thought of another revolution. The industrious classes had strong reasons for preferring almost any peace to a renewal of war, almost any government to a return of anarchy. The nation, therefore, though it did not love the restored dynasty, would in all probability have made no movement for the purpose of subverting it. But there were two parties resolutely bent on the expulsion of the royal house, – the republicans and the soldiers.

The soldiers had been rejoined by 150,000 of their comrades, who had been prisoners of war in Russia and England, and were again ready to give battle to all the world. In no portion of the community was the antipathy to the Bourbons so strong; in no portion of the community were the feelings which restrain men from attacking established government so weak. The circumstances under which the restoration had taken place were humiliating to the nation; but they were doubly humiliating to the army. The nation looked with aversion and contempt on the emigrants; but no where was that aversion and contempt so strong as in the army. All its great captains were new men, – men who, under the old system, would have passed their lives in the ranks, – but whom the revolution had covered with orders and placed on the steps of the throne. The new dispensers of honours and rewards were persons from whom the utmost that could be expected was, that they should forgive those great actions which had so long excluded them from their country, – persons to whom the bridge of Jena and the pillar of Austerlitz were eye-sores, and to whom the news of that terrible retreat, in which 100,000 brave warriors had died of cold and hunger, was the dawn of hope. The institution of the Swiss guard had been revived, – an institution which could not but be most offensive to every Frenchman in the military profession. Old nobles, who had never borne arms, or who had borne them only against France, were appointed to command men who had made the name of France terrible to all the kingdoms of Europe. The French nation had great blessings to set off against the evils of the restoration: but those very circumstances which were blessings to the nation were curses to the army. The merchant and the cultivator might rejoice in the return of peace; but the soldier, inured to danger, pining for excitement, burning for revenge, ambitious of promotion, was already sick of his inglorious repose. Political liberty, utterly unknown under Napoleon, had been, to a considerable extent, granted by Louis. But the soldier is a slave among freemen, and a freeman among slaves. In a nation which has a liberal form of government he lies under a double restraint, – that imposed by military discipline, and that imposed by constitutional jealousy. Under an absolute government, he is indemnified for the bondage in which his superiors hold him, by the license in which he is indulged when off duty. The independence of the judges was nothing to the soldier: he was under the jurisdiction of a court-martial. The guarantees given to personal liberty were nothing to him: his commander could at any moment place him under arrest. The prospect of absolute monarchy had no terrors for him; and was in the highest degree exhilarating, if the absolute monarch was to be his father Violet, his own little corporal, – the chief who, while deposing kings and imprisoning popes, had condescended to pull the mustachios of his veterans, to drink out of their bottles, and to taste their ammunition-bread.

The republican party, though small, contained men of great talents and high reputation. The gloomy energy of the imperial government had kept them down; their movements had been dodged by the police; their speculations had been mutilated by the censors; the lustre which had belonged to their names during the early part of the revolution had waxed faint, and become obscure, when confronted with the effulgence of one too dazzling reputation. The power which had restrained them had fallen; and they were now again formidable. They hated and feared the Bourbons. They had no love for Napoleon: but, without the help of the army, it was impossible to expel the Bourbons; and, without employing the name of Napoleon, it was impossible to procure the help of the army.

The republicans committed, undoubtedly, a very great error, – an error at least as great as any of those with which they justly reproached the royalists. It was natural and right that the friends of liberty should watch with jealous attention the measures of the restored dynasty. Some of the proceedings of the government had been blamable; the language of some of its adherents was exasperating. The charter had defects: one of its most salutary and important provisions had already been violated. But, on the other hand, the system of society which the revolution had established remained untouched in its essential parts. There was great reason to hope that even the most violent royalists, when the excitement produced in their minds by the restoration had subsided, would see their own weakness, and the immense strength of the interests which they were assailing, and would quietly abandon the hopeless project of restoring the old privileges and revoking the national sales. The revolution had, in its infancy, triumphed over the monarchy, the aristocracy, and the church, then in their full vigour. In its youth, it had beaten off the emigration, when the emigration had all Europe at its back. It was now strong, not only with that strength which had belonged to it as a revolution, but with all the added strength of legitimacy and prescription. It was formed into an established system of law; it was confirmed by the royal charter; it was intimately connected with every thing in the state; it was interwoven with all social and domestic relations; – was it likely that it would now be vanquished by enemies so few and so contemptible, that, a few years before, common observers had not been aware that they even existed as a party?

Louis had bestowed on France some blessings, which the republicans should have valued more highly than they seem to have done. There was a free tribune; there was, to a certain extent, a free press. Above all, there was peace; and peace, carefully maintained, could not fail to be prolific both of knowledge and of liberty. But the strongest reason for preferring the Bourbons to Bonaparte was, that the Bourbons were weak, and that Bonaparte was strong. The very fact that the army detested the royal family, was a reason which should have led every liberal politician to stand by that family.

There were evils, undoubtedly, in the existing state of things; but the life of a statesman is merely a choice between evils. The question was not between the Bourbons and a perfect government, but between the Bourbons and Bonaparte, – between the Bourbons and the man who had made a legislative assembly leap out of the windows of St Cloud at the point of the bayonet; who had fettered the press; who had silenced the tribune; who had filled France with spies; who had erected state prisons, as dark and secret as the Bastille. Nor was the choice merely between the Bourbons and Bonaparte. The Bourbons and peace were on the one side, Bonaparte and a general war on the other. In such a war, defeat would endanger the independence of France. Every victory which she might obtain would be a victory over her own liberties. If the French armies were defeated, the Bourbons would come back armed with new powers, furnished with new pretexts, and exasperated by new injuries, to attack the order of things which the revolution had established. No person, on the other hand, could be so weak as to think that Napoleon would submit to constitutional restraints from inclination. If he were to return to Paris, after making a campaign as splendid as that of Austerlitz, after annihilating the kingdom of the Netherlands and restoring the boundary of the Rhine, would he lie under the necessity of submitting to such restraints? Would not his old guard follow him as resolutely into the hall of a representative chamber as against a line of Prussian or Austrian soldiers? Would not the nation be found as submissive in the time of his triumphs as it had been in the time of his reverses? That young soldiers should be impatient to efface the shame of defeat and invasion was natural; but men, who called themselves philosophers and friends of the human race, should have remembered at what a price nations sometimes purchase military renown.

Unhappily, the republicans consulted their passions rather than their reason. The king would not have been a despot if he could, and could not have been a despot if he would. Napoleon, raised to the throne of France, would have both the inclination and the means. But Louis was the representative of the emigration, and Napoleon of the revolution. The men of the revolution, with a levity inexcusable in persons conversant with public affairs, preferred a vigorous, crafty, and remorseless tyrant, with a tri-coloured cockade, to a prince whose disposition was liberal, and whose government, though by no means faultless, was the best that they had ever known, but who wore a blue riband, and claimed the throne by a hereditary title.

Such was the state of France. The body of the nation, though dissatisfied with the government, shrank from the thought of another revolution; and, though irritated by the recent invasion, shrank from the thought of another war. The zealous republicans hated the restored dynasty so much, that, in order to expel it, they were ready to bring back Napoleon and war. The army adored Napoleon, and considered war as in itself a blessing.

On the 1st of March, 1815, Napoleon landed with a few followers on the coast of France, near Fréjus. When the news arrived in foreign countries, he was generally supposed to have ventured on this enterprise in despair and weariness of life; but the event soon showed how accurate an estimate he had formed of his own powers, and of the state of feeling in the army.

He advanced to Grenoble. During his march through Dauphiné, the peasantry received him with acclamations. The higher orders, who had more to risk, stood aloof. Grenoble was garrisoned by about 3000 troops. One of the regiments quartered there was commanded by a young man whose courage had already made him eminent among soldiers, and whose handsome person and light accomplishments made him the idol of the most brilliant drawing-rooms of Paris, – Colonel Labédoyère. Though both the family from which he sprung, and the family into which he had married, were distinguished for their zeal for the house of Bourbon, he had conceived a fanatical attachment to the cause and person of Napoleon. The ardour of his soldiers seconded or outran his own. As soon as the emperor appeared, the outposts threw down their arms. Labédoyère flung away his white cockade, and placed a tricoloured riband in his hat: his example was followed with shouts of joy by his own regiment. The rest of the garrison arrested the commandant. An eagle, which had been concealed since the restoration, was brought forth from its hiding-place, and substituted for the royal flag. The emperor entered the city in triumph, and found himself again at the head of an army.

He advanced on Lyons. A considerable force was stationed there under the command of the brother of the king; but the aspect of the troops clearly indicated that no reliance could be placed on them. The count of Artois went round the ranks; he addressed the soldiers one by one; he stooped to caresses and supplications. It was in vain: – 'You must excuse us, sir,' said one veteran, covered with wounds and military decorations; 'you cannot expect men to fight against their father.' The prince fled with a single attendant; and Napoleon was received with enthusiasm by those who had been sent to withstand him.

At Lyons he published a series of decrees, framed with great dexterity, in such a manner as to identify his personal cause with that of the revolution. He thus gave a definite shape and a grave sanction to the vague fears of the new proprietors and the muttered discontents of the army.

By one of these decrees he directed that all the badges of the Bourbons should be pulled down, and replaced by the emblems of the revolution. By another, he annulled the law which had restored the unsold estates. By a third, he abolished the feudal titles which Louis had revived. By a fourth, he banished from the French territory all those emigrants who had not been erased from the proscribed list before the return of the king. He revoked all the military commissions which the king had given to emigrants; and abolished the Swiss guard.

With respect to the political institutions which he proposed to establish, he was less explicit: he merely directed the electoral colleges to assemble in a grand council of the field of May at Paris, for the purpose of revising the constitution of the empire.

This was the first time since the day on which the states-general assumed the title of the national assembly, that any of the old institutions or historical names of France had been employed on the side of the revolution. The majority of the people were, probably, not aware that the council of the field of May had ever existed; and its constitution was not perfectly known even to antiquaries. There was, however, a certain propriety in reviving it on the present occasion; it was the only ancient institution which had no connection with the house of Bourbon, or with the privileges of the old nobility. The field of March was the general assembly of the Franks under Clovis and his immediate successors. Under the later Merovingians it fell into disuse. Pepin restored the authority of the great national council, and gave to it the name of the field of May. It repaid his services with the crown of France. In 752, it deposed the feeble Childeric, and placed the mayor of the palace on the throne. It met frequently during the splendid reign of Charlemagne. It was in the council of the field of May that the restorer of the western empire declared war against the Lombards. It was in the council of the field of May that he received the homage of the Saxons. That institution decayed, as it had risen, with the Carlovingian dynasty. The central authority of the state became weak, and the authority of petty princes succeeded to it. The great conventions of the nation fell into disuse, as the feudal system waxed strong. The elevation of Hugh Capet was the decisive triumph of the feudal system. Eight hundred years later, the unhappy descendant of Hugh Capet perished under the ruins of the feudal system. The name of the field of May could not, therefore, but have a pleasing sound to a man who was the enemy of feudal privileges, and the competitor of the third race, who had held his crown by a title similar to that of Pepin, and who had extended his authority over dominions as vast as those of Charlemagne.

Napoleon continued his march towards Paris: one army was posted at Melun, to oppose him in front; another, under the command of Ney, was collected at Besançon, to attack him on the flank. Of all the generals who had served under the emperor, Ney had, perhaps, the most brilliant reputation. In the art of conducting the great operations of war, indeed, he was inferior to Masséna, to Soult, to Suchet, or to Davoust; but in action his eye was quick, and his dispositions prompt and judicious. His personal valour was pre-eminently conspicuous, even in an army abounding with brave men. He was one of those who at Fontainebleau had urged Bonaparte to abdicate; and he had every reason to think that, by his conduct on that occasion, he had forfeited the favour of his old master. He had offered his services to the king; and when he was requested to repair to Franche Comté, and to collect an army from the garrisons in that part of France, he readily consented, and pledged himself to bring Bonaparte prisoner to Paris. In the promises which he made he was in all probability quite sincere; but he knew not what he promised. He tried all his influence on his troops; but they were obstinately resolved not to fight against the emperor. At first the marshal swore that he would take a musket and begin the attack himself. This was no more than he had repeatedly done during the retreat from Moscow; nor was it from any fear of personal danger that he did not now keep his word: but, brave as he was in war, he was weak and irresolute in council. The soldiers murmured against him. Napoleon wrote to him in the most flattering and caressing language. He hesitated, yielded, and declared for the emperor. To save the Bourbons was indeed out of his power; but he might have saved his own honour and that of the French army, which could not but suffer from the perfidious conduct of a soldier so high in rank and in reputation.

The emperor marched to Auxerre. The troops quartered at that city had already assumed his colours. Here he was joined by the army of Franche Comté, under the command of Ney, and pushed forward rapidly towards Paris.

The last army of the Bourbons was stationed at Melun. It was known at that place, on the 20th of March, that Bonaparte had passed through Fontainebleau. The troops were drawn up in order of battle to oppose his progress. He came – not at the head of his soldiers, but in an open travelling carriage, escorted by a few light cavalry. He rode up at once to the front of the line. In a moment the white flags were torn down; the white cockades were trampled under foot; and the remonstrances and orders of the royalist officers were drowned in a rapturous shout of 'Long live the emperor!'

All was now over. Louis had fled to the Low Countries during the preceding night. Late in the evening of the 20th, Bonaparte entered Paris. He was received, as the king had been received eight months before, with gloomy indifference by the majority of the people. Few of the respectable inhabitants of the southern suburbs left their houses; and those who appeared in the streets gave few signs of exultation. But the soldiers thronged round their chief in a mood widely different from that in which they had, ten months before, attended the carriage of the infirm king. When they reached the Place du Carousel their acclamations redoubled. In that ample space were assembled the most zealous adherents of the emperor. Soldiers and citizens were mingled together, shouting and weeping with joy. As the carriage stopped they pressed round the door; they kissed the hand of the restored exile; they embraced him; they smothered him with their embraces; they bore him aloft in their arms; and so, in a triumph prouder than ever conqueror had enjoyed, amidst flaring torches and waving caps, and brandished swords, he rode on the necks of that stormy multitude through the doors of the Tuilleries, and up the great staircase into the royal chambers.

The revolution was now complete. In several parts of France the royalists attempted to make a stand in favour of the house of Bourbon. They were every where overpowered; and the authority of Napoleon was fully re-established over the whole country.

In the restoration of Bonaparte, as in the restoration of Louis, the nation had been passive. Louis had been restored by a handful of royalists, and by the allied armies: Bonaparte was restored by a handful of republicans, and by the French army. The French people, indeed, have always carried to an excess their fondness for what is brilliant and theatrical in politics; and no enterprise was ever more brilliant or more theatrical than that in which Napoleon had now succeeded. But even the admiration excited by so signal a proof of his courage and genius could not wholly reconcile his subjects to his return. They remembered his long tyranny. They looked forward to a general war; to the certain consequences of war, – vast levies of men, and the destruction of trade; and to the possible consequences of war, – defeat and subjugation. They were proud of the valour and of the great actions of the army. But they had not forgotten its licentiousness, its insolence, and the invidious privileges which it had enjoyed under the reign of a military sovereign. They shrank from the thought of hostilities, the result of which would inevitably be, either a foreign invasion or the re-establishment of the imperial despotism in all its ancient vigour. It was only by close union at home, that they had any chance of preventing an attack from abroad. Many wise and virtuous men, therefore, who had opposed the enterprise of Bonaparte, and who deeply regretted its success, thought it their duty to support his government. Of these M. Constant was the most distinguished. That upright and eloquent statesman had exerted himself strenuously to uphold the cause of the Bourbons, as long as the conflict remained undecided. When, however, the royal family had been expelled, he gave in his adhesion to the imperial government, and took an active part in the formation of the new constitution. He was, accordingly, charged by the royalists with scandalous inconsistency. History will probably pronounce that his conduct, though inconsistent in seeming, was perfectly consistent in substance; that he was faithful to the interests of the state, and indifferent to the names and titles of its rulers. It was better for France that the Bourbons should continue to reign, than that Bonaparte should be restored. But when Bonaparte had been restored, it was better for France that he should reign in peace, than that the nation should engage in a war in which it would either be conquered by strangers, or enslaved by its own sovereign. No good Frenchman could wish to see the Bourbons restored by foreign conquerors: and there was a far greater chance that Bonaparte might be kept within the limits of a constitution in a time of peace than in a time of military success. To prevent Europe from attacking France was, therefore, the first object of every patriotic and reflecting citizen; and that Europe might abstain from attacking France, it was necessary that France should present a firm and unbroken front to Europe.

But the allies had already taken their resolution; – a resolution, which, according to all the principles of public law acknowledged by the civilised world for ages, was perfectly just, and which the great body of mankind, who judge of counsels only by the event, will always consider as prudent. All the states of Christian Europe declared war against Napoleon; and certainly, if in any case a war for the purpose of preserving or redressing the balance of power be justifiable, they had the right on their side. The balance of power would not have been so much deranged by any accession of territory which France could have made as by the restoration of Napoleon. Louis, with the Rhine and the Ticin for a boundary, would have been a far less formidable neighbour than Napoleon with the diminished empire over which he now reigned. Danger from the extent of the country which a sovereign rules; danger from the importance of the military positions which are at his command; danger from his chance of obtaining a large addition to his dominions by inheritance, – all these dangers have been deemed good grounds of war. The danger arising from his personal character, from his ambition, his perfidy, his activity, his capacity, his valour, may be a

97

danger no less real, and no less pressing than any other. The most celebrated war which had ever been waged in Europe for the purpose of maintaining the balance of power was that in which England, Holland, and the empire engaged, for the purpose of excluding Philip of Anjou from the throne of Spain. It can scarcely be denied that the personal character of Napoleon gave stronger reasons for apprehension than the domestic connections of Philip; that the probability that Napoleon would add to his dominions by conquest was much stronger than the probability that Philip would add to his dominions by inheritance.

The war of 1815 belongs to the same class of wars with the war which the ministers of Anne carried on against the house of Bourbon, and is broadly and clearly distinguished from those wicked and disgraceful wars with which it has sometimes been confounded, – that which Austria waged against liberty in Naples, and that which the faction of Villèle waged against liberty in Spain. To settle the interior government of France was not the primary object of the allies. The claims of Louis XVIII were to the coalition of 1815 what the claims of the archduke were to the coalition of 1701, – a mean, and not an end. To make war on Bonaparte merely because he was an usurper, would have been the height of iniquity. But if the governments of Europe thought him, as they had good reason to think him, a most powerful, most crafty, and most obstinate enemy of the independence of all nations, they were not bound to leave him in possession of power, because they could not deprive him of power without interfering in the internal concerns of France. It is true, that wars for the purpose of averting evil not absolutely present and certain have been far too common in Europe; but, of all wars of precaution, the war of 1815 will probably be considered by impartial men as that for which the strongest case may be made out.

The allies had indeed lost much of that moral force which had been on their side during the campaigns of 1813 and 1814. In 1792, and during many subsequent years, there had been a conflict in the public mind between the desire of improvement and the respect for antiquity. Those who, in any part of the continent, were eager for the removal of abuses looked with hope to the French republic. Those who were solicitous for the safety of existing institutions regarded that republic as the scourge of mankind; but in 1813 all difference was at an end. There

98

was against France, throughout the whole civilised world, a coalition of opinions and feelings as vast and as formidable as the great coalition of governments. In the British parliament there was as little opposition to the war as in the cabinet itself. Even the citizens of New England celebrated the downfall of the tyrant with magnificent public banquets, and extolled the despotic sovereign of Russia in terms such as his own senate might have employed. All political sects were knit together in a confederacy against a man who was the deadly enemy both of liberty and of old establishments. But this confederacy, as it had been produced by danger, was dissolved by success. The arrangements of the congress of Vienna bitterly disappointed all judicious and benevolent men. In those arrangements there was, it is true, nothing new or peculiar, – nothing for which precedents, sanctioned by respectable names, might not be pleaded. The partition treaties which William III concluded with Louis XIV were as objectionable as any thing that was done in 1814 and 1815. In 1735, the great powers of the continent terminated their disputes by placing a Pole on the throne of Lorraine, and settling on a northern prince the reversion of Tuscany. In making these dispositions they paid not the least regard to the wishes of the people of whom they were disposing; and yet their conduct had never been censured on this ground. But Europe was not what it had been. Nations were no longer in a mood to be transferred, like flocks of sheep, from one proprietor to another. The feelings which the allies outraged were precisely those feelings to which they had, during their struggle with Bonaparte, been compelled to appeal, – those feelings which had saved their own families from the fate of the houses of Orange and Bourbon, – those feelings which had broken the yoke of Germany, and had kept alive during six years the spirit of resistance in Spain. It was immediately after stimulating to its utmost point the enthusiasm of national feeling, that the potentates sat down to the work of partitioning. In their new distribution of territory, all differences of manners, of laws, of religion, of language,

[one page missing]

In the mean time, Napoleon was occupied in providing for the military defence of his empire, and in preparing a new plan of government. He had, by one of the decrees which he promulgated at Lyons, directed the electoral colleges to meet in the council of the field of May for the purpose of revising the constitution. He now resolved to take a different course, and to change the fundamental laws of the empire by his own authority. The council of the field of May was to meet merely for the purpose of swearing fidelity to the constitution given by the emperor.

The new scheme of government was set forth in an instrument called the 'additional act.' Almost all the provisions of this law were borrowed from the royal charter. Like the royal charter, it emanated from the authority of the sovereign alone. Every objection, substantial or formal which could be made to the system established by Louis, applied equally to that established by Napoleon. There could be no oppression more odious to the revolutionary party than that of hereditary peerage. Nothing in the system of the old monarchy had been so unpopular as the privileges of blood. None of the acts of the constituent assembly were remembered with so much gratitude as those which had established social equality. It was the pleasure of Bonaparte, however, that a hereditary chamber should be part of the new constitution; and the republicans acquiesced. The new plan was submitted to all the citizens in their departments. Very few persons ventured openly to declare their dissent. The new [constitution?][7] was ratified, as the consular constitution [of 1804][8] had been ratified by a great majority of those [who voted?].[9] More than 12,000,000 persons signed the additional act. Of these about one-fifth part were in the army or the navy.[10]

The emperor formed the ministry in such a manner as to give to the revolution what the revolutionists considered as a strong guarantee. Two of the highest situations in the government were filled by men who had sate on the benches of the Mountain, and concurred in the regicide vote; but who in every other respect differed from each other as widely as it was possible for human beings to differ. These men were Carnot and Fouché.

Carnot had participated less in the crimes of the revolution, and had been more fondly and deeply attached to its principles than almost any other member of the jacobin party. As one of the committee of public safety he had affixed his signature to many atrocious resolutions. But it is asserted that he took no part in more revolutions beyond the performance of this formal act.[11] His sincerity, his disinteredness, his courage, the eminent services which he had rendered to the republic as a director, and the intrepid manner in which he had opposed the ambitious projects of Bonaparte, as a tribune, had atoned for the support which in times of violent excitement and great public danger he had given to the terrorists. Since the restoration he had done more than any other person to inflame the public mind against the Bourbons. He now lent all the weight of his character and of his influence to the cause of the emperor; and though he strongly disapproved of that provision of the additional act which established a hereditary chamber, he shewed his fixed resolution to support the new government by accepting a peerage.

Fouché had gone deep into the worst crimes of the reign of terror, without even the deplorable excuse of fanaticism. He had shewn himself equally unscrupulous as a democrat and as a courtier. He had, during the former reign of Napoleon, been placed at the head of the imperial police, the worst part of that iron tyranny under which the liberty of action and thought had been so sternly kept down. When the Bourbons returned, he attempted to make his peace with them, and was repeatedly consulted by the king. The republicans extended to his conduct the same indulgence which they extended to that of the emperor, and for the same reason. Fouché was one of the men of the revolution. He had sprung from it; he had served it; he had given pledges to it. The revolutionists were therefore willing to forget that the emperor had been the most despotic of masters. Indeed, during this unhappy year, they seem to have been into a kind of political supralapsarianism, – a fixed persuasion that the elect of the revolution could never fall away, and that the reprobates of the emigration could never be converted. Fouché repaid their superstitious confidence by commencing a private correspondence with the ministers and generals of the allied sovereigns.

The convention of the field of May did not take place till the 1st of June. It met for the purpose not of deliberating, but of exhibiting a magnificent spectacle to the people of Paris. The emperor in his own name, and the electors in the name of the French people, swore fidelity to the new constitution. On the 3d of June, the chamber of representatives sat for the first time. The representatives were chosen by the same electoral colleges which had formerly returned the candidates for the legislative body. This was by no means a good consistency. Still the new chamber was the first assembly which, since the return of Bonaparte from Egypt, had been freely elected by a large body of people. Here appeared, after a long retreat from public life, the brave and humane La Fayette, the most distinguished of the constitutionalists of 1791. There appeared Lanjuinais, the noblest relic that poison and hunger, wild beasts and the guillotine had left to France, of the brilliant and ill-fated Gironde. No man had raised his voice more boldly for the life of the king; no man had contended with more spirit and eloquence against the Jacobins for the liberty of the convention; no man had more firmly opposed in the senate the tyranny of the emperor. In this representative chamber some men, whose names have since been renowned through Europe, made their first public appearance. M. Dupin and M. Manuel peculiarly distinguished themselves by their eloquence and ability.

The conduct of the assembly indicated, if not a republican spirit, yet at least a strong constitutional jealousy of the executive power, – a jealousy which, when we consider the danger impending over France from without, we may be inclined to pronounce excessive, but which, when we consider the character of the man to whom the executive power was entrusted, appears only reasonable. The situation of the representatives was one of extreme difficulty, and the most favourable construction ought to be put upon their conduct. They had two objects, – to strengthen the hands of the emperor against Europe, yet to keep his hands weak against France; and it may be doubted whether it was possible to attain either of these objects without prejudice to the other.

The emperor wished the representative chamber to place his brother Lucien in their chair. Their choice, however, fell on Lanjuinais; and their discussions took the turn which might have been expected from such a choice. It was moved that the title of deliverer of the country should be conferred on Napoleon. The proposition was rejected with derision. One member brought forward a motion against titles of honour. M. Dupin denied the right of the sovereign to give a constitution to France by his own authority, and proposed a resolution purporting that the oath of the field of May did not preclude the legislature from revising the additional act. These motions were not carried; but that they should ever be proposed and discussed seemed to Napoleon the height of insolence. In private he spoke with extreme bitterness of the most distinguished representatives; and even in his public communications with the chamber he could not wholly conceal his feelings.

Between the opening of the session and the departure of the emperor for the army only a week elapsed; yet that short time was long enough to shew that between Napoleon and liberty there could never be more than a short and uneasy suspension of hostilities. A war with all Europe, and the imminent danger of invasion, could not produce, even for five or six days, the decent semblance of concord between the parties whom an unnatural coalition had bound together. Suspicions covertly hinted on one side and refinements more openly given on the other, made up almost the whole intercourse between the representative chamber and the throne. It was impossible to doubt, that as soon as the frontier of France had been placed in a state of security, the legislature would be dissolved. Such were the advantages which some ill-advised patriots had purchased by a revolution and a general war.

An event which at the time seemed the most overwhelming disaster that ever France had sustained, but which has ultimately conduced far more to her prosperity than a series of campaigns as brilliant as those of 1805 and 1806 would have done, put a terrible close to the dispute between a tyrant who was making a tool of liberty, and those friends of liberty who flattered themselves that they would make a tool of an able and resolute tyrant. On the 12th of June, Napoleon announced to the representative body his intention of instantly setting out for the army. He charged them to abstain from discussions which might tend to shake the public confidence in the new form of government, and to defer the consideration of abstract questions till the real dangers of the state should have passed by. As he spoke he darted a flame of fire through the ranks of the opposition. The representatives retired from his presence irritated, yet overawed. The same night he left Paris for the frontier.

In a week he returned, pale, gasping for breath, and sinking under the fatigue of his body and the emotions of his mind. He had staked every thing; and every thing was lost. His army was dispersed; his guard was cut to pieces; his artillery was taken. A hundred and fifty thousand enemies, elated by victory, were pouring along the Sambre into Artois.

Military history has seldom been well written by any but military men; and no part of military history has been more darkened by controversy than the history of the campaign of 1815. With respect to the leading events of that campaign there is, however, no obscurity. It is universally allowed that Napoleon fully supported his high reputation. On the 15th of June he attacked the Russian outposts. On the 16th he defeated the army of marshal Blücher in a general engagement. On the 17th, after making arrangements which, as he conceived, secured him from any molestation on the part of the Prussians, he marched against the English, whom his dispositions had prevented from giving any assistance on the preceding day to their allies. The duke of Wellington, who had received an assurance from marshal Blücher that, if the English army were attacked, the Prussians would come to its support, resolved to risk a battle for the preservation of Brussels. He took up a position at Waterloo, in front of the forest of Soignies; and here, on the 18th of June, was fought the memorable battle which fixed the destinies of Europe.

From ten in the morning till seven in the evening the French continued to attack with that characteristic impetuosity, which has often decided in a single onset the fate of a campaign; and the English to stand their ground with that characteristic resolution, which is never so composed and so stubborn as towards the close of a doubtful and bloody day. At the very moment at which the last and most desperate charge of the French was beaten back, the columns of marshal Blücher appeared. The whole English line advanced. The French army broke up and fled in utter confusion. The old guard alone turned desperately to bay; and, hemmed in on every side by overwhelming numbers, perished in a manner worthy of its long and terrible renown. Ney fought on foot sword in hand, till he was swept down [by?] the stream of fugitives. The pursuit continued during the night. Seven thousand prisoners and more than two hundred guns were taken by the conquerors. The number of the French who were killed or wounded was beyond all estimation. Those who escaped were scattered in every direction; and no force capable of making the

[one page missing]

government, at the head of which Fouché was placed. In the chamber of peers Lucien Bonaparte insisted on the rights of his nephew. Labedoyère spoke on the same side with vehemence almost frantic, but his voice was drowned by murmurs. Massena silenced him by a grave and commanding rebuke, and he left the tribune muttering curses of rage. In the chamber of representatives it was moved that Napoleon the Second should be proclaimed; but the majority received the proposition coldly. M. Manuel, in a speech of great eloquence and dexterity, moved the order of the day, and this amendment was adopted.

While the legislature was engaged in these discussions, the invaders were advancing with terrible rapidity. On the 21st of June they entered France. Cambray fell on the 24th: Peronne on the 26th. On the 29th the duke of Wellington crossed the Oise; and on the 3d of July the English and Prussian armies appeared before the barriers of Paris.

Marshal Davoust, who commanded the garrison of the capital, concluded a military convention with the foreign generals, and retreated with all his forces behind the Loire. On the 4th of July the allied armies entered Paris, and on the 8th Louis arrived . . .

NOTES TO MACAULAY'S TEXT

1. 1795 is the correct date.
2. Of course the reference is to the famous books by Rousseau and Montesquieu.
3. Places at which Louis XVIII stayed while in exile, Mittau in Russia and Hartwell House near Aylesbury in Buckinghamshire.
4. The massacre of St Bartholomew, 1572.

5. Louis issued his proclamation at St Ouen, just outside Paris.

6. This is a paraphrase of the royal declaration issued 3 May 1814.

7. 'ocno o vn': a line in ink is drawn through these letters. The type was disturbed, and the letters 'stitutio', which apparently belong here, appear in the next line immediately below.

8. 'ı stitutio'; a line in ink is drawn through these letters. The type was disturbed, and the numerals 804, which apparently belong here, appear in the next line below. If the passage refers to the constitutional change that made Napoleon First Council for life, the correct date is 1802. This change in the constitution was endorsed by plebiscite in which there was a vast majority.

9. 'ho804ted'.

10. The correct results of the plebiscite were 1,305,206 votes yes, 4,206 no, and at least 5,000,000 abstentions: Jacques Godechot, *Les Constitutions de la France depuis 1789* (Paris, Garnier–Flammarion, 1970), p. 228.

11. The passage has been altered from: 'But it is asserted that he took no part in more revolutions beyond the performance of this formal act.'

BIOGRAPHICAL GLOSSARY

ARTOIS, comte d': see Charles X.

BARÈRE, Bertrand (1755–1841). The son of a propertied family, he was educated at Toulouse for a career in the law. He voted for the death of Louis XVI, and later turned against Robespierre. He served Napoleon, and in 1815 he was driven, as were other regicides, into exile. He returned to France after 1830.

BILLAUD-VARENNE, Jean-Nicolas (1756–1819). An unsuccessful lawyer and itinerant teacher in the 1780s, Billaud-Varenne was known as a radical well before the Revolution. He joined the Jacobin club in 1789 and later was elected to the Convention. He was soon known as an extremist ally of the Mountain and a spokesman for the Hébertistes. He was appointed to the Committee of Public Safety in 1793. Together with his friend Collot, he forced Robespierre to turn against Danton, and he later conspired with the coalition which overthrew Robespierre. Tried and convicted with Collot by the Thermidorean Convention, he was deported to French Guiana in April 1795. In 1800 he turned down Napoleon's offer of a pardon. In 1817 he moved to Haiti, where he died two years later.

BLACAS, Pierre Louis, duc de (1771–1839). Emigrating when the Revolution began, he fought in varied *émigré* and allied armies. He served in diplomatic missions for Louis XVIII before the restoration. Having become a royal favorite, he returned to France with the king and during the first restoration he was among Louis's closest advisers. His unpopularity led to demands for his resignation from all offices, and after the second restoration he was mainly occupied with diplomatic missions to Italy. After the July Revolution he went into exile.

BONAPARTE, Lucien (1775–1840) was the most able of Napoleon's brothers. Although during Napoleon's absence from Paris Lucien defended his reputation and interests, a coolness developed between the brothers. He served as Napoleon's ambassador to Madrid. When Napoleon returned to Paris after Waterloo Lucien advised him to not abdicate and to dissolve the assembly and seize complete powers. After 1815 he retired to Italy.

BRISSOT, Jacques-Pierre (1754–93). A literary and idealistic young man, Brissot quit his training in law in 1780 and launched himself into journalism. Having gained a reputation as a critic of the monarchical constitution, Brissot was elected to the Legislative Assembly in 1791 and soon became leader of the 'Brissotin' (later known as the 'Girondist') faction. Although successful in discrediting the king and declaring war against Austria, the Girondists' predominance was shaken by the new elections to the Convention, the trial of the king, and Gen. Dumouriez's defection. After the Insurrection of June 1793 the Convention arrested Brissot. He was tried and guillotined with several of his friends.

CAPET, Hugh (938–96), founder of the Capetian dynasty.

CARNOT, Lazare (1753–1823). Trained in military engineering, he earned a reputation as a mathematician and capable officer, but was excluded from advancement because of his *roturier* origins. He was elected to the Legislative Assembly in 1791 and to the Convention in 1792, and he designed the Convention's *levée en masse*. Appointed to the Committee of Public Safety in 1793. His reputation as the organizer of victory saved him from the anti-Robespierrist reaction. He was elected to the Directory in 1795. Although opposed to Napoleon, he served him under the Empire and again during the Hundred Days. After the second restoration he was exiled as a regicide.

CHARLES X (1757–1837). As a brother of Louis XVI he became an *émigré*. As the *comte d'Artois* he vigorously supported the claims of the old monarchy and the Church. During the reign of Louis XVIII he was a hero of the Ultras. He succeeded to the throne in 1824 on the death of his brother. Although his reign began with his professions of liberalism, his repressive policies provoked liberal and republican opposition. After the July Revolution he again went into exile.

CHILDERIC III (d. 754), the last Merovingian king of the Franks.

CLOVIS (c. 466–511), defeated the last Roman ruler of Gaul and then united the various Frankish tribes of northeastern France. He converted to Christianity c. 498.

COLLOT d'HERBOIS, Jean-Marie (1749–96). A professional actor when the Revolution began, he became a member of the Jacobin club. He was elected to the Convention in 1792 and showed himself a radical opponent of the Gironde and Danton. Along with Billaud-Varenne, Collot was regarded as a leader of the Hébertistes – those who believed in drastic egalitarian social change. He was a member of the Committee of Public Safety, and soon afterwards he was sent to direct the mass executions of the Lyonnais. Bitter at Robespierre's soft line on dechristianization and property redistribution, Collot helped bring about Robespierre's fall. During the anti-Jacobin reaction he was tried and convicted for this ruthless conduct, and he was deported to French Guiana, where he died of yellow fever.

CONDÉ, Louis-Joseph de Bourbon (1736–1818). He emigrated in 1789 and raised an army of *émigrés* in Germany. From 1792 to 1814 he persistently fought the revolutionary and Napoleonic armies.

CONDORCET, Marie-Jean, Marquis de (1743–94) was a member of the Academy of Sciences, a protégé of d'Alembert, and he helped prepare the *Encyclopédie*. Elected to the Legislative Assembly, he was one of the first to declare for a republic and for calling a national convention. However, he was opposed to the execution of the king and the arrest of the Girondins, for which he was outlawed. While in hiding he wrote the *Esquisse d'un tableau historique des progrès de l'esprit humain*. He died in prison, perhaps by suicide.

CONSTANT de Rebecque, Benjamin (1767–1830). Born in Lausanne, young Constant studied in Germany and England. A moderate supporter of the French Revolution, he decided in 1794 to settle in Paris with his friend Mme de Stael. He soon became well known as a defender of political and economic liberalism and an apologist for the Directory. After Napoleon's coup Constant was appointed to the tribunate. Expelled in 1802 for his vocal opposition to Napoleon's rule, in 1803 he followed de Stael into exile in Switzerland.

Constant wrote novels, literary criticism, essays on romanticism and religion, and tracts attacking Napoleon. In 1814 he returned to Paris and during the Hundred Days he surprisingly accepted Napoleon's proposal that he draft a new, liberal constitution. Fleeing to England after Napoleon's final defeat, Constant returned to Paris and was elected as a liberal Independent to the Chamber of Deputies in 1819. He was an eloquent and impassioned opponent of the ultras, and in 1830 he led the Left's opposition to Charles X's dissolution of the Chamber. Louis-Philippe appointed him president of the Council of State in 1830.

COUTHON, Georges (1755–94). A provincial lawyer and noted academician in the Auvergne, Couthon was elected to the Legislative Assembly in 1791 and soon became an important figure in the Jacobin club. Elected to the Convention in 1792, he joined the Mountain in advocating death for the king and introducing the motion to proscribe the Gironde. Appointed to the Committee of Public Safety, he helped Robespierre transform the Committee into an effective center of executive power. As a *représentant en mission* in southern France in 1793, Couthon directed the Convention's military victory over the federalists in Lyon. In 1794 he helped initiate the Reign of Terror in Paris. Considered, along with St-Just, to be Robespierre's closest ally, Couthon was among the first to be guillotined after the coup of Thermidor.

DANTON, Georges (1759–94). Trained to be an attorney like his father, be began his career as *avocat* of the *Conseil du Roi*. He became a popular leader in the Jacobin club, and in 1791 he was elected to the Legislative Assembly. Under attack by the Girondists, he sided with the Mountain. He directed the first Committee of Public Safety, but declined to serve with Robespierre on the second. Late in 1793 he spoke out against the extreme Hébertistes. In 1794 he was arrested, tried, and guillotined.

DAVOUST, Louis-Nicolas (1770–1823). He trained for a military career, and although the son of a noble family, in 1790 he led his regiment in a pro-revolutionary revolt. Forced to resign in 1793, he was recalled after Thermidor. He served Napoleon with distinction and retired when Napoleon abdicated, but returned during the Hundred Days. After Waterloo, he signed the Convention that gave over Paris to the allies.

DUMOURIER, Charles-Francois du Perier (1739–1823). The son of a military family, he joined the army in 1758, served with distinction in the Seven Years War, and was sent on diplomatic missions by Louis XV. He joined the Jacobin club in 1790 and swore loyalty, first to the constitutional monarchy and then to the Convention. In 1793 he tried to lead his army against the Convention in Paris, but the soldiers refused to follow, and he defected to the Austrians. He lived the remainder of his life in exile, for neither the Directory, nor Napoleon, nor Louis XVIII would allow his return to France.

DUPIN, Andre-Marie (1783–1865) had a distinguished career as a lawyer. He served as a liberal deputy during the last years of the Restoration, supported the July Revolution, became a close adviser to Louis Philippe and was president of the Legislative Assembly during the second Republic, yet he allied himself to Napoleon III before the coup of 1851.

DUPONT, General Pierre-Antoine (1765–1840). Although he received high praise from Napoleon for his achievements in central Europe, for his disappointing performance in Spain Napoleon had him tried and stripped of his rank. After Paris fell in 1814 he was made provisional minister of war by the allies, and this was confirmed by Louis XVIII. He made himself unpopular by demobilizing the imperial officers corps and by granting honorific rank to returning *émigrés*, making it necessary for the king to replace him with Soult. He later sat in the Chamber of Deputies as a liberal until 1830.

EBROIN (d. 680), chief of the palace in the Frankish kingdom of Neustria. He wielded power while Theodoric was king. After defeating Pepin of Austrasia he was assassinated, and this marked the end of Neustrian influence in Frankish politics.

FÉNELON, François (1651–1715), tutor to the duke of Burgundy, archbishop of Cambrai, and author of *Aventures de Télémaque* (1699).

FOUCHÉ, Joseph (1758–1820), was the son of an overseas merchant in Nantes. Elected to the Convention in 1792, he was part of the Mountain. In his provincial mission as a representative of the Convention he was an advocate of dechristianization, and in Lyon he helped Collot d'Herbois organize the mass execution of civilians. He took part in the Thermidorean coup, but was impeached in 1795. Resurrected as minister of police in 1799, he held this post until 1802 and again from 1804 to 1810. He was responsible for the censorship, espionage, and repression of opposition under Napoleon. He served again as minister of police during the Hundred Days, but also played an important part in preparing for the king's return and the second restoration. He served in the new government for one year until, after the election in 1816, he was expelled and as a regicide was forced to emigrate.

GUADET, Marguerite-Elie (1755–94) was a native of the Gironde and an *avocat* in Bordeaux. Elected to the Assembly in 1791, he joined in the Jacobin attack on the Feuillants, calling for the seizure of *émigré* property and the deportation of priests. He took part in the attack on the Tuileries (20 June 1792) and denounced Lafayette in the Assembly. However, he later became affiliated with Girondists against the Mountain. With other Girondists in June 1793 he was proscribed. He fled from Paris but was arrested, tried, and guillotined.

HENRY IV (1553–1610), founder of the Bourbon dynasty. He entered the religious wars in 1568 on the Calvinist side. Defeated in war, he decided to abjure Calvinism and in 1572 married the sister of Henry III, Marguerite de Valois. Four years later he left the Catholic court and renewed the conflict. After Henry III was murdered in 1589 he tried to establish himself as a Calvinist king. Unsuccessful, he again gave up Calvinism, saying 'Paris is well worth a mass,' and in 1594 he was crowned at Chartres. By guaranteeing religious toleration with the Edict of Nantes in 1598, he reunited France and put an end to the religious wars. He was assassinated by one Ravaillac, a Catholic and a fanatic.

LABÉDOYÈRE, Colonel Charles (1786–1815). After joining the army as an officer in 1806, he served in several campaigns with distinction. After being wounded for the third time, he returned to Paris in 1813, where he married the daughter of an old royalist noble family. Under Louis XVIII he accepted a regimental command and was stationed at Grenoble. When Napoleon returned from Elba, Labédoyère rallied his troops under the imperial eagle and in return was promoted to general rank and made a peer of the empire. He was among the last to retreat at Waterloo and in the chamber of peers he spoke in vain against Napoleon's abdication. Wandering in the south, he decided to bid a last farewell to his wife in Paris before emigrating to America. He was recognized, arrested, and executed. The first officer to defect to Napoleon in 1815, he was also the first to be officially punished.

LAFAYETTE, Marie-Joseph, Marquis de (1757–1834), the son of an illustrious noble family. In 1777 he went to America as an official adviser to the American revolutionary army. Reinforced with French troops, he helped force Cornwallis's surrender at Yorktown in 1780. Back in France he became famous as an aristocratic reformer. Elected to the noble assembly in the Estates-General in 1789, he played a leading role in its deliberations. By 1791, however, he was politically isolated and retired from his command of the National Guard. As commander of the northern army in 1792 he tried to lead his troops against Paris, but when his troops mutinied he defected to the Austrians. From 1814 to 1824 he sat in the Chamber as a liberal deputy, and in 1830 he led the revolutionary National Guard during the July revolution.

LAINÉ, Joseph-Louis-Joachim (1767–1835), an *avocat* from Bordeaux, was elected to the legislative body in 1808. In 1813 he criticized Napoleon's failure to seek peace and his mismanagement of the economy, and this led to his dismissal. He took part in the royalist rebellion in Bordeaux in March 1814. He was elected president of the Chamber of Deputies in 1814. During the Hundred Days he emigrated, returning to preside over the Chamber in 1815, where he was leader of the right-center faction. He served as minister of interior under Richelieu and proposed the new electoral law which was intended to weaken the ultras. He was made a peer in 1825 and retired from politics after the July revolution.

LANJUINAIS, Jean Denis (1753–1827). An acknowledged authority on ecclesiastical law, he was widely known for his expert criticism of feudal rights and canon law. He was elected to the Third Estate of the Estates-General in 1789 and emerged as an advocate of the civil clergy and the one-house constitution. Elected to the Convention, he defended the Gironde and the due process of law. Among the deputies proscribed in June 1793, he fled to Rennes and hid until November 1794. Napoleon appointed him to the Senate in 1800. In April 1814 he voted for Napoleon's abdication; Louis XVIII, in return, made him a peer. Lanjuinais agreed to preside over Napoleon's Chamber of Representatives during the Hundred Days, but because he obligingly dissolved it after the allied invasion, Louis was later constrained to maintain him as a peer. Until his death Lanjuinais was a liberal dissident in the House of Peers, an opponent of censorship, property compensation for *émigrés*, and Ultramontanism.

LOUIS XVII (1785–95). The death of his older brother in 1789 made him the dauphin. His mother's execution in 1793 made him the legitimate Bourbon king. Imprisoned with his family during his father's trial and again in 1794, he fell sick and died aged ten.

LOUIS XVIII (1755–1824). He became an *émigré* in June 1791. After the execution of Marie Antoinette he announced himself regent for his nephew Louis XVII, after whose death he proclaimed himself king. He wandered in Russia, Prussia, and England until the first restoration, and went to Ghent during the Hundred Days.

LOUIS-Philippe (1773–1850). The eldest son of the duc d'Orleans, on inheriting this title he became head of his branch of the Bourbon family. He fought in the revolutionary army until 1793 when, in view of the dangers experienced by the royal family, he fled, thus beginning a twenty-one year period of exile, which ended with the first restoration. During the Hundred Days he was in England. The July revolution made him king of the French, which he continued to be until 1848.

LOUIS, Joseph-Dominique (1755–1837). As a specialist in finance he held various ministerial offices in 1814 and again after the second restoration. He supported the July Revolution and held office until 1832.

MANUEL, Jacques-Antoine (1775–1827). An *avocat* from Provence, he first entered political life as an elector to Napoleon's Representative Body during the Hundred Days. Later during the restoration, his Bonapartist reputation and his membership in the revolutionary Carbonari caused him to be excluded from the bar. Elected in 1818 as a liberal independent to the Chamber of Deputies, he allied himself with Constant in attacking the ultras' reactionary legislation. In 1823, he became the center of a cause célèbre when he delivered a speech opposing French intervention in Spain, which so infuriated the ultras that they voted that he be excluded from the Chamber. He was carried bodily out of the hall by guards and never returned to politics.

MARAT, Jean-Paul (1743–93). Apart from his birth in Neuchâtel, little is known of Marat's early years. In the 1770s he emerged in London as a doctor and pamphleteer. Appointed physician to the personal guards of the comte d'Artois from 1777 to 1783, Marat also wrote several scientific studies but was ostracized from the *Académie des Sciences* for his radical politics. In 1789 he began publishing the journal *L'Ami du Peuple* and soon became a hero among Parisians for his defense of popular sovereignty and his vicious attacks on the aristocrats, the monarchists, and the clergy. Elected to the Convention, he sided with the Mountain against the Girondists, who tried unsuccessfully to convict him of sedition. Marat was murdered in 1793 by Charlotte Corday, a young royalist from Caen.

MARIE-LOUISE de Hapsbourg-Lorraine (1791–1847), daughter of Francis I of Austria and Marie-Thérèse of Naples. Soon after his divorce from Josephine, Napoleon married Marie-Louise (1810) in hopes of producing a male heir for the Empire and strengthening his alliance with Austria. In 1811 she gave birth to a son, Napoleon-Francis (entitled 'the king of Rome'). After sending her away from Paris with Napoleon-Francis in March 1814, Napoleon abdicated to Elba without ever seeing either of them again. Made the duchess of Parma (1816–31) by the Treaty of Fontainebleau, Marie-Louise became the mistress of the Austrian general von Neippurg, by whom she later had three children. Having abandoned the king of Rome to her father and Metternich in Vienna, she secretly married Neippurg after Napoleon's death.

MARMONT, Auguste Viesse de (1774–1852). The son of a military family, Marmont entered the French artillery in 1792 and at the siege of Toulon (1793) made a favorable impression on Napoleon, who made him his aide-de-camp and promoted him general while fighting in the Egyptian campaign (1798). Marmont commanded a corps on the retreating western front and on 30 March 1814 he engaged the allies in a fierce battle on the outskirts of Paris. Days later Joseph Bonaparte and Talleyrand persuaded him to withdraw from Paris towards the north, an action for which Napoleon, now forced to abdicate, considered him a traitor. Marmont was made a peer later that year and was forced into exile with Louis XVIII during the Hundred Days. A supporter of Charles X during the July Revolution, he was forced into permanent exile in Italy after 1830.

MASSÉNA, Marshal André (1758–1817). Raised as an orphan, Masséna enlisted in a French royal Italian regiment in 1775, was elevated to captain in the revolutionary army, and was made division general in 1793. As Napoleon's most trusted lieutenant in the Italian campaigns, he showed a genius for speed and maneuver, winning a key victory at Rivoli (1797). Masséna later performed brilliantly and was made field-marshal in 1804. Sent to Portugal later that year, he was defeated in two major battles and had to be replaced by General Marmont. Though his popular reputation remained intact, Masséna was never again trusted by Napoleon. After the Hundred Days, Masséna rallied to the cause of the restoration.

MASSILLON, Jean-Baptiste (1663–1742), the celebrated preacher at the court in Versailles, achieved great popularity among the Parisians for his moving sermons.

MIGNET, François (1796–1876), a liberal historian who played an important role in the journalistic politics leading up to the July revolution. He came to Paris in 1821, where he was a successful lecturer. He was fascinated by seventeenth-century English history and used it as an analogy in his interpretation of French events since 1789. He was a lifelong friend of Thiers, and together, with Carrel, they founded and edited the influential *National*. Mignet was a leader of journalistic opposition to Polignac's ordinances.

MONTESQUIEU, Charles-Louis Secondat (1689–1755). The son of an óld aristocratic family, he became a lawyer and served as deputy president of the Bourdeaux *parlement* before writing, among other works, the famous *Lettres persanes* (1721) and *Esprit des Lois* (1748).

MONTESQUOIU (-FEZENSAC), l'abbé François-Zavier (1757–1832). A noble by birth, a cleric by profession, he had a place at court before the revolution. He was a deputy of the Parisian clergy at the Estates-General of 1789. Known as a moderate and for his willingness to give up some clerical privileges, he also was an eloquent defender of the clergy. He became an *émigré* from 1792 to 1795. In 1814 he helped prepare the Charter and became minister of the interior. During the Hundred Days he retired to England, and on his return to France in 1815 he was made a peer.

NEY, Marshal Michel (1769–1815). Son of a blacksmith, Ney ran away from home to join the Hussars in 1788. He distinguished himself in the revolutionary wars (1792–4), was made a general in 1793, and first met Napoleon when the latter was first consul in Paris in 1801. During the Empire he was an indispensable leader in almost all Napoleon's campaigns. In 1814 he convinced Napoleon to abdicate and then took an oath of loyalty to the Bourbon throne. In March 1815, on hearing of Napoleon's return from Elba, Ney promised to bring him back 'in an iron cage,' but soon he defected to the emperor's cause and was given high command during the Waterloo campaign. After Napoleon's final defeat Ney was arrested, tried, convicted, and executed. A man of humble origins, great bravery, and no political ambition, Ney was considered a martyr in the eyes of later Bonapartists.

ORLEANS, duc d'. See Louis-Philippe.

PEPIN of Herstal (*c.* 640–714), an Austrasian magnate, mayor of the palace of Austrasia. At first defeated by Ebroin in 680, Pepin defeated the Neustrians after Ebroin's death and became a kingmaker and effective ruler of the Franks.

PEPIN le bref (*c.* 715–68), the second son of Charles Martel. After his father's death, since his brother adopted monastic life, Pepin acquired his father's effective power over the Frankish kingdom. Anointed as king by the pope in exchange for his defense of papal interests.

PHILIP of Anjou (1683–1746), founder of the Bourbon dynasty in Spain. As the son of the dauphin and Marie Anne of Bavaria (granddaughter of Philip IV of Spain), the duke of Anjou was the legitimate heir to the Spanish throne, which was confirmed by the Spanish king Charles just before his death. When Philip after receiving the Spanish crown also insisted on retaining his right to the French throne, the War of Spanish Succession (1702–13) became inevitable. By the treaty of Utrecht he was forced, amongst other things, to renounce his French claims.

REYNOUARD, François (1761–1836). An academician and *avocat* for the *parlement* of Aix before the Revolution, Reynouard was elected to the Legislative Assembly in 1791 and, though he took little active part in its affairs, he was imprisoned in 1793 for his ties to the Girondin faction. Released on 9 Thermidor 1794, Reynouard returned to his native Provence and began a noteworthy career as poet, writer of historical tragedies, and philologist. Chosen twice (1806, 1811) to serve in the Legislature, he showed an independence of mind, and in the summer of 1814, when the same body convened as the new Chamber of Deputies, he protested against the royal ministers' strict views regarding censorship. In 1815 Reynouard quit politics and devoted himself to the study of medieval Provençal poetry.

RICHELIEU, Armand-Jean du Plessis (1585–1642), minister of Louis XIII and political architect of French royal absolutism. Born to a noble family which had served the monarchy with distinction, young Richelieu studied theology and was appointed in 1608 as bishop of Lucon, and later became cardinal. He was the first French bishop to implement the reforms of the Council of Trent. In 1624 he became chief of the royal council.

ROBESPIERRE, Maxmilien (1758–94). A popular young lawyer and judge in the 1780s, Robespierre was known in his native town of Arras as a brilliant academician and a protector of ordinary people against aristocratic privilege. He was elected to the Estates-General in 1789, and after the National Assembly was dissolved in September 1791 he became a leader of the Jacobin club. He achieved a reputation as an orator and meticulous organizer. He opposed the military elite and the Brissotin war policy, and in September 1792 he was elected to the republican Convention. On the strength of his popularity the Mountain succeeded in destroying the Gironde, and this led to his appointment in July 1793 as effective head of the Committee of Public Safety. In this position Robespierre suppressed further popular unrest and led the Convention to victory over foreign allies and domestic opponents. By spring 1794, however, it was feared that he was using revolutionary ideology to promote personal dictatorship. On 27 July 1794 (9 Thermidor) a coalition of his enemies managed to order his arrest in the Convention. Unable or unwilling to call on the Paris Commune for help, Robespierre and more than 100 of his followers were guillotined.

SANTERRE, Antoine Joseph (1752–1809). A native of Paris and a brewer by profession, Santerre emerged as a leader of the Parisian *sansculottes* early in the Revolution. He took an active part in the storming of the Bastille and the attack on the Tuileries. He was appointed commander of the Paris National Guard by the Insurrectionary Commune. In May 1793 he was sent by the Convention to direct its military campaign against the Vendéan royalists. After being appointed commander-in-chief of the western armies in August, Santerre was defeated in battle, recalled to Paris, and imprisoned by the Convention in September. In July 1794 the Thermidorean Convention released him and dismissed him from the military.

SAINT-JUST, Louis-Antoine de (1767–94) trained as a lawyer, he became an ardent revolutionary. After his election to the Convention in 1792, he emerged as the fearsome leader of the Mountain's verbal offensive against the king and the Gironde. As a deputy *en mission* in Strasbourg, the Rhine, and Belgium, he became famous for his puritanical and egalitarian reforms of the French Military. In 1793 (aged 25), he was appointed to the Committee of Public Safety, where he helped Robespierre consolidate executive power until the coup of Thermidor (27 July 1794) when he was guillotined.

SIEYÈS, Emmanuel-Joseph (1748–1836) had a clerical education and began his career with respectable ecclesiastical appointments. His middle-class origin was an obstacle to advancement, and this encouraged his interest in the political theories of the *philosophes*. As a deputy for the Third Estate at the Estates-General of 1789, he achieved instant fame for his revolutionary pamphlet, *What is the Third Estate?* He continued to play an important role in the Assembly in 1790, but found his monarchist opinions increasingly attacked after the death of his ally Mirabeau in April 1791. Although elected unwillingly to the Convention, Sieyès carefully avoided political activity from August 1792 until Thermidor (July 1794). In 1795 he reentered the affairs of the Convention and, having helped design the intricate Constitution of the Year III, was elected to the Council of Five Hundred in October 1795. In 1799 he won a seat on the Directory and conspired with Napoleon and Ducos in the coup of 18 Brumaire. Although his newly drafted constitution was neglected and his enjoyment of effective political power soon came to an end, Sieyès remained in government as a senator. In 1804 Napoleon entered him into the Legion of Honor and in 1808 made him count of the Empire. Banished during the restoration as a regicide, Sieyès returned to Paris after the July Revolution and died there six years later.

SOULT, Marshal Nicolas-Jean de Dieu (1769–1851). Although he began his army career as an enlisted infantryman, by 1794 he had achieved the rank of general. In 1804, after serving in Italy and Switzerland, he was appointed field-marshal by Napoleon, and in 1805–6 he played an indispensable role in the German–Austrian campaigns. Soult was sent in 1808 to Spain, where he was engaged for years against Spanish guerrillas and English regulars. A brilliant strategist, he managed to delay for many months the advance of Wellington's superior forces into southern France (1813–14). During the first restoration Soult swore loyalty to the Bourbon throne and in December 1814 became minister of war. Yet during the Hundred Days he served Napoleon as chief-of-staff, and went into exile after the second restoration. He was recalled to France in 1819 and made a peer in 1827. After the July Revolution he held various offices.

SUCHET, Marshal Louis-Gabriel (1777–1826). An officer in the National Guard during the Revolution, by 1798 he was promoted to the rank of general. He distinguished himself at Austerlitz and Jena. After achieving two victories in Spain (1810–11) he was made field-marshal in 1811. As commander of the army of the Midi he signed the armistice with Wellington in 1814. Although he was given a peerage by Louis XVIII in 1814, he rallied to Napoleon during the Hundred Days.

STAËL-Holstein, Mme Germaine de (1766–1817), novelist, playright, critic, political essayist, and celebrated for her salon, was the daughter of the Swiss banker and Minister of Finance Jacques Necker. In 1786 she married the Swedish ambassador in Paris, Baron de Staël-Holstein. She was known for her beauty, literary sensitivity, and fervent liberalism. From 1794 to 1803, between repeated periods of exile, she attracted the most famous *lumières* to her Paris salon. Although at first she welcomed Napoleon, the two came to dislike each other. In 1803, Napoleon effectively banished de Staël from France; in return she wrote tracts attacking the Empire and with Benjamin Constant founded the famous salon at Coppet. Traveling frequently in Germany, Mme de Staël was much impressed by German romanticism and lent her support to growing nationalist opposition against Napoleon's pan-European system. Back in Paris in 1816, she fell ill and died there the following year.

TALLEYRAND-Périgord, Charles-Maurice de (1754–1838), bishop, politician, and ambassador during several regimes, a man of great diplomatic skill. The son of a noble family; educated for the Church; made bishop of Autun in 1788; elected to the Estates-General in 1789, where he endorsed the abolition of tithes and feudal dues and the nationalization of the Church. He led a diplomatic mission to England in 1793 but failed to prevent war, for which he was denounced before the Convention, leading him to choose temporary exile. Served as foreign minister for the Directory and for Napoleon after his coup. While still serving Napoleon he secretly prepared for the Bourbon restoration. Made foreign minister by Louis XVIII, he played a leading role at the Congress of Vienna. He was ousted from power during the second restoration, but he intrigued against Charles X and helped secure the throne for Louis-Philippe. Served as ambassador in London for four years before his last retirement in 1834.

VERGNIAUD, Pierre-Victurnien (1753–93). A native of the Gironde, Vergniaud studied law in Paris and returned in 1781 to become an *avocat* for the *parlement* of Bordeaux. Known as a warm supporter of the Revolution, he was elected to the administration of the *département* of the Gironde in 1790. In the following year he was elected deputy to the Legislative Assembly. During his first months in Paris, Vergniaud emerged as an eloquent spokesman of the Girondist faction, advocating war against Austria and attacking the king's foreign policy. In July 1792, however, he sensed the danger of a popular rebellion and tried secretly but in vain to compromise with the king. It was Vergniaud who led the futile Girondist effort to save the king's life. Following the Insurrection of June 1793 the Convention listed his name among the 29 Girondist leaders to be arrested. Vergniaud made no attempt to flee. He was condemned by the revolutionary tribunal and guillotined with twenty other deputies.

VILLELE, Jean-Baptiste (1773–1854). After serving as a naval officer in the West and East Indies, he returned to France in 1807 with a large fortune from an estate on the island of Réunion. He was appointed mayor of Morville, near his native Toulouse. In 1813 he joined the royalist secret society *Chevaliers de la Foi* and in 1814 took part in the royalist uprising in Toulouse. After election as mayor of Toulouse and member of the Chamber of Deputies in 1815, he emerged as a prominent spokesman for the ultra-royalists. He was one of the founders of the *Conservateur*. He held various ministerial offices during the 1820s, including presidency of the Council, and had a large part in arranging the military expedition to Spain (1823), the compensation for confiscated *émigré* property (1825), and the stricter censorship (1827). After failing to gain sufficient electoral support in the 1827 elections, he resigned in January 1828. After the July Revolution he retired from politics.

VOLTAIRE, François-Marie Arouet de (1694–1778), dramatist, historian, critic, poet, satirist, and the most celebrated of the *philosophes*. Voltaire spent his early years in Paris and London, supporting himself by writing and by accepting political patronage. Already a familiar name in the courts and salons of Europe by 1740, he traveled constantly between France, Belgium, Switzerland, and Prussia. He performed occasional diplomatic services and was until 1753 on intimate terms with Frederick II of Prussia. Expelled from Geneva in 1758 for his contribution to the *Encyclopédie*, he settled in Ferney, in France, where he held a salon and continued to write on controversial topics. He returned in 1778 to a triumphal welcome in Paris, dying there months later aged 84.

TABLE

The following table gives the page and line numbers in the present edition, in italics, of the first lines of each page in the corresponding text as printed in the copy in the archives of Longman Group Ltd.

1	*43:1*	32	*58:23*	52	*75:1*	71	*91:14*
8	*43:18*	33	*59:17*	53	*75:31*	72	*92:8*
9	*44:25*	34	*60:11*	54	*76:25*	73	*93:4*
16	*45:22*	36	*61:6*	55	*77:19*	74	*93:35*
17	*46:18*	37	*62:1*	56	*78:15*	75	*94:30*
18	*47:11*	38	*62:33*	57	*79:9*	76	*95:25*
19	*48:6*	39	*63:27*	58	*80:6*	77	*96:19*
20	*48:16*	40	*64:22*	59	*81:1*	78	*97:14*
21	*49:8*	41	*65:17*	60	*81:32*	79	*98:8*
22	*50:3*	42	*66:11*	61	*82:27*	80	*99:2*
23	*50:33*	43	*67:6*	62	*83:22*	82	*99:34*
24	*51:28*	44	*68:1*	63	*84:17*	83	*100:30*
25	*52:24*	45	*68:32*	64	*85:12*	84	*101:26*
26	*53:20*	46	*69:27*	65	*86:7*	85	*102:20*
27	*54:15*	47	*70:23*	66	*87:3*	86	*103:16*
28	*55:10*	48	*71:18*	67	*87:34*	87	*104:11*
29	*56:5*	49	*72:13*	68	*88:30*	89	*105:8*
30	*56:35*	50	*73:9*	69	*89:25*		
31	*57:28*	51	*74:5*	70	*90:20*		